BATS, PADS AND CIDER
A Miscellany of Somerset Cricket

*"There! You see? It's always like that with these
West Countrymen; they bowl superbly for an hour or so,
and then they begin to think about apples."*

CB Fry (Cricketer, diplomat and writer, 1872-1956).

CHARLES WOOD

Illustrated by the author

HALSGROVE

For my sons Lawrence and Felix

First published in Great Britain in 2011

Also by Charles Wood:
How to Survive in Somerset
Surviving Another Somerset Year
Charles Wood's Somerset Quiz Book
Exmoor Amour

Publisher's Disclaimer
As is well known, Halsgrove have disowned Mr Wood on many occasions
in the past and this particular volume is no exception. The views expressed
herein arise entirely from the fevered brain of Mr Wood who remains
entirely responsible for them, the Publisher is pleased to say.

British Library Cataloguing-in-Publication Data
A CIP record for this title is available from the British Library

ISBN 978 0 85704 065 7

HALSGROVE
Halsgrove House,
Ryelands Business Park,
Bagley Road, Wellington, Somerset TA21 9PZ
Tel: 01823 653777   Fax: 01823 216796
email: sales@halsgrove.com

Part of the Halsgrove group of companies
Information on all Halsgrove titles is available at: www.halsgrove.com

Printed and bound in the UK by the MPG Books Group

The Naming of Parts

Acknowledgements

My grateful thanks must go to Vic Marks for the road miles once spent together and for his stoicism at my driving. Such thanks must also extend to Mervyn Kitchen, Brian Rose, Andrew Caddick, and Mark Lathwell for having taken the time to chat in odd places, to the late Eric Hill for the wonderful memory of press box hospitality, and to Peter Roebuck for once buying me lunch.

Special gratitude as well to Felix for keeping me up to date with cricketing trifles, to Bugsy of the buttercups, to Roy of the *Three Ferrets*, to Snatch and Grab, to carpenter Phil, to Trevor of bat and poultry, and also to my loving wife who, having come to avidly learn the rudimentary rules of cricket, has held me steadfast to the writing of this book through her endless encouragement.

My thanks also to the cat for sharing the excitements of cricket radio commentaries that have inevitably caused key-pad tapping delays. And, as a consequence, I additionally thank my publishing editor Steven Pugsley for his patience, and regret the need for his frequent nudges over past months.

Most importantly of all, I thank Somerset County Cricket Club and the cricket lovers of the Summer Land who make the long days of warm sunshine so special for match day scribblings in a 'Moleskine'.

Wiveliscombe, Winter 2011

A Trying Top Order

Of Openers and Slip-Ups

"What do they know of cricket, who only cricket know?"
C.L.R. James (Afro-Trinidadian cricket writer, 1901-1989).

Long ago Glastonbury Tor was known as 'Ynys Witrin', the Isle of Glass, but it was somewhat later that the town became known to some as 'Tor-ville' where by common knowledge batting was fragile, and slips weren't just reserved for being behind the wicket and the outside edge. On the profes-sionalism issue at least, Somerset's cricketers had skated on thin ice.

Let it be said, however, that it's been an age now since Somerset last played 'home' cricket at 'Tor-ville'. These days, becoming scruffy in grass stained whites is primarily reserved to exertions in the Deane, with just an occasional outing to Bath.

The last time the men of Somerset put on whites in Glastonbury the music Festival wasn't the extravaganza it is today, and 'Tor-ville' had lain artisti-cally fallow for a few years. In fact, it had done so ever since Nicolas Roeg and David Puttnam had released their *Glastonbury Fayre,* filmed at Worthy Farm's 1971 solstice gathering; a movie that captured the likes of David Bowie, Hawkwind and Melanie, as well as traditional music and poetry.

And although '70s outsider folk regularly came Glastonbury way to immerse themselves in the Arthurian and to buy hippy tut, the Summer Land's cricket lovers came in their droves, hopeful of bat music and the poetry of motion.

Yet there was no great expectation of such arty displays coming from the home side. This fact is best illustrated by the true tale, occasionally whispered in dark corners aided by a stiff 'Grouse', or for that matter several pints of scrumpy, about a Somerset batter who in a desperate attempt to avoid being struck by an intimidating delivery, overbalanced and collapsed into his wicket. Batsman, bat and stumps were all being laid out flat together in hopeless confusion. Still dazed, the unfortunate picked himself up, seized one of the stumps in mistake for the bat and stumbled away with it in the direction of the pavilion– surely a record mode of dismissal, and so very Somerset.

And then there was the Brian Lobb incident. At Glastonbury during the '50s, Brian Lobb, a tall gangling right-arm fast-medium bowler – the greatest number 11 of all time some say, well, certainly the most entertaining – tottered back to the pavilion after having his trousers pulled down to 'flagpole' by team-mates pratting about at the end of one happy match.

To be fair to Brian as one who could take a jape his fielding was forever the subject of amusement. "He changed course a dozen times while the ball trickled straight to him at long-leg," wrote Somerset's historian, David Foot. When batting he turned ungainliness into an art form and he was also a poor judge of a run. Brian's obituary in the 2001 Wisden prints the Somerset man's own words: "I once got run out by deep mid-on, who overtook me as I unwisely strolled to the other end".

For perhaps a century the County had been composed of some yokels, some not very good players, and some odds and sods, among them a Ceylon tea-planter, a future admiral, several lawyers and clergymen, a Bastard, a Granny, a Prince of Cooch Behar, and CJR, 'the White Mouse'.

Perhaps Greg Chappell had been the first player to bring the element of being 'world-class' into the club. But he was only there for a couple of years at the end of the '60s, and on his departure things had reverted back to 'situation normal'.

Any artistry on show seemed to be exhibited purely from within the ranks of visiting teams. And as popular attractions went Yorkshire were right up there. So, unsurprisingly, long before being renamed the 'Tor Leisure Ground' – an overdue recognition of proximity to the iconic Somerset hump that's topped by St Michael's roofless tower – there was a gurt crowd at the Morlands Athletic Ground.

They had come in numbers bearing picnic baskets, cider bottles, tobacco pouches and boxes of Swan Vestas for one of those Sunday games when sponsors still made cigarettes, and bowlers were restricted to fifteen yard run ups, something that, perhaps, assisted them to not run out of puff.

The New Zealander Tom Lowry would have been in his element. Here was a chap who played some games for Somerset, although his qualification to do so was obscure. The story is told that his birthplace was said to be Wellington, without mentioning that it was not the Somerset market town but the one in New Zealand. While at Cambridge Tom was a member of a 'Hellfire' club, having qualified for it by blowing three smoke rings and spitting through them.

Dudley Carew, a gentleman of traditionalist leaning, would surely have turned in his grave. Not only merely at Tom's antics but at matters even more ghastly. In his book *To the Wicket* published in the early 1950s he had opined with angst about a 'secret society'. Led by 'the little man' the 'society' was making insidious plans to change the face of Dudley's beloved game. What was it that had got Dudley's conservative gander up? Simply the notion of limited overs cricket. Seeing himself as a knight in shining armour, Dudley pledged to put a stop to such nonsense and believed that he would not be alone.

"Cricket has got to have the courage of its own aristocracy," Dudley wrote. "Few things before the war were more insidiously dangerous than the cult of the 'little man'.

"He, the 'little man', stood for a fatuous complacency, a morbid self-satisfaction, an entire and monstrous unwillingness to concern himself with anything that did not immediately touch his hire-purchase comfort. Anything to save himself the trouble of thinking, anything which made no demand upon his spirit, his brain, or his stunted sense of loveliness – quick results and flashy action were his motto.

"To turn cricket into a cross between rounders and tip-and-run is as much an insult to the boy who bowls to a wicket chalked against a brick wall as it is to the man who has his initials printed in front of his name on the score card – and the sooner those who profess to care for the game at the same time as they put forward plans which would turn it into a caricature of itself realise that simple fact the better."

Oh, what a dinosaur Dudley turned out to be, although to be fair, 'Crusoe' Robertson-Glasgow, Somerset's Scots born pre-war right-arm fast-medium bowler who turned humorous broadsheet journo, echoed Dudley a tad more succinctly by describing one-day cricket as "the new clockwork monkey (that) delights for a few hours."

"Hey, Geoffrey! Why don't ee cum an' play fer us?" shouted a pipe-smoking, banana-munching, Brylcreemed wag of small stature, loudly.

Standing on the boundary edge at long leg, Geoffrey Boycott having earlier hit 82 not out turned his head slightly a few yards away from where I was huggered up with my parents and replied from the corner of his mouth, "You could never afford me down 'ere."

As Dad gazed with reverential awe, Boycs had spoken the truth. Somerset had already broken the piggybank to entice former white-roser Brian Close to skipper the county, hopefully to bring steel to their game and to attempt to teach a professional attitude not related to money or fitness.

So, our Geoffrey, the 'Greatest Living Yorkshireman', an opener of undisguised ego, sort of summed things up really. Somerset was just an impoverished rural club lacking ambition. "Unfashionable plodders" were the words Dad used to describe them.

One of the match umpires, the craggy, sensitive, Aussie-born Bill Alley, southpaw welterweight, dancehall bouncer, manual worker and former Somerset player would have perhaps had something to say about that.

Yes, Bill was a shooter of rabbits, a sinker of pints, a player of skittles and a keeper of sheep, but with the help of cherished cross-batted fours and sixes he was the last county player to top 3,000 runs in a season. Bill's age had always been a matter of good-humoured debate and he had kept the mystery going, picking up a few cheques from the national papers on the strength of it. He was also a man to whom Geoffrey, believing he'd be captaining Yorkshire, had once popped a question. Namely, would Bill like to join them?

"I wish I'd asked him to put it on paper," Bill had later remarked. But that was all past history.

Dad scanned the Somerset names on his scorecard. "Rose, Denning, Botham, Kitchen, Burgess, Dredge, Moseley. "Hmm, never heard of any of them."

I was surprised, even I had heard of Mervyn Kitchen as being rather a fine batsman, although getting on a bit. However, it was my first time of seeing him in the flesh, and indeed of seeing the whole unheralded bunch. Yes, I liked cricket a lot and devoured many a cricketing article, but always found myself lured away from matches to dangle for river trout, a bit like Guy Earle the hard-hitting Somerset batter from the 1920s. However, my fishing licence had expired and Dad didn't want me "summonsed for poaching". My saying that I was no Arthur Wellard went straight over Dad's head.

And not only did Arthur play merry hell with nature's larder he was also a man who deserved respect by generating money for nothing. Playing against

Middlesex in 1936 he damaged a ball beyond repair pinging it against a corrugated fence on edge of the River Tone. As it was Arthur who hit it, the ball sold for two shillings and sixpence.

Of course the trivialities of Arthur were of no interest to my Dad. A Yorkshireman to his core, all he had wanted was to get a clear look at Geoffrey rather than making do with grainy black and white images on the telly. Mum tagged along dutifully to immerse herself in her knitting.

Dad, however, seemed a mite nonplussed by the other larger than life Yorkshireman, 'Closey' present. Maybe it was because the Colossus of Rawdon, or the "bald old blighter" as Alan Gibson called him, had deserted his Yorkshire roots. But what was he supposed to have done? Yorkshire had sacked him. Reportedly he was constantly raging in the dressing room. Apparently though that was rubbish. He was either drinking tea or whisky.

Many years later Peter Roebuck would describe Closey as "a gambler on the field". This was code to mean he was a good captain for three-day cricket but "not so hot" in one-dayers. In one-day games it's good when nothing happens. Closey would always try to make something happen. By all accounts he did do some crazy things on the field like putting Mervyn on to bowl when Mervyn didn't even bowl in the nets resulting in the ball disappearing out of the ground.

I'm sure Mervyn would have taken it all in good grace. Having scored bucketfuls for Flax Bourton as a teenager and become a hero around the lanes of his native Nailsea, by 1973 he had evolved into a much loved Somerset veteran of the punch and pull, prompting John Arlott to pay apt tribute in Mervyn's benefit brochure that year:

"Some cricketers seem to personify their counties and to see Mervyn Kitchen in the field or at the crease is to recognise him as a Somerset man. His rosy red face, humorous expression, ample seat, rolling walk and rich accent are unmistakably those of a West Countryman."

On that blue-skied, sun-kissed day in the summer of 1976 Closey got lucky with his decision making, much helped by Mervyn's contribution, though one obviously made with the bat.

"Hey Geoffrey, fancy an ice cream cone?" shouted the Brylcreemed wag, as Boycs adjusted his cap and trotted to retrieve a ball that had passed him by. Lashed his way by Mervyn it had nestled against the wag's colourfully striped picnic chair. "Fred never used to say no to an ice cream fieldin' where yer stood now. One hand fer the ball, one fer the ice cream, that was Fred Rumsey."

Boycs made no verbal response other than to give an exasperated sigh. Any thoughts Boycs may have had about the summer habits of his former England team-mate during the mid 1960s and Somerset's most casual of left-arm fast-medium pacers, he kept to himself.

Soon after Boycs had chucked the ball back in the direction of the wicket, to Dad's almighty chagrin, Somerset won. And I had an epiphany.

Sadly, there was a footnote – Tom Lowry passed away, aged 78, two days after the match.

Full on the boot! Why can't the beggar bend?
I hope it sets his beastly corns alight,
And, as he waddles to the other end,
He'll tell the Captain all about his sight,
And how the wicket-keeper made a snatch
And queered his view, and how I bowled too soon –
As if it wasn't just the sort of catch
A child would hold, at midnight, with no moon.

Full on the boot again! The batsmen run
Their all-decisive single, swift as deers;
The Umpires pluck the bails, the match is won,
But not by us; on my impatient ears
There strikes a voice instinct with self-content,
"The light was very bad and growing worse,
The wicket-keeper ———" So I turned and rent;
"You're far too fat, and fatness is a curse;
You never bend, and if you did, you'd fall;
You really never ought to field at slip –
In fact, you never ought to field at all.
If some instructor taught you how to skip,
And kept you skipping for a year or so,
You might, with fortune favouring, obtain
A minor post in Betram Mill's show,
But never darken Cricket's door again."

*   *   *

Next Saturday I took an easy catch
Full on the boot, at slip – we lost the match.

RC Robertson-Glasgow

A Reason For An Epiphany

SOMERSET v YORKSHIRE

John Player League 1976
Morlands Athletic Ground, Glastonbury on 18 July 1976 (40-over match)
Somerset won the toss and decided to field
Umpires: WE Alley, WL Budd.

Yorkshire innings

*G Boycott	not out	82
JH Hampshire	c Close b Moseley	5
JD Love	b Burgess	16
CM Old	not out	82
Extras (10 b, 9 lb, 1 w)		20
Total (2 wickets, innings closed, 40 overs)		205

Fall of wickets: 1-11, 2-64

Did not bat: PJ Squires, +DL Bairstow, GB Stevenson, P Carrick,
HP Cooper, GA Cope, AL Robinson.

Somerset bowling: Moseley: 8.0.31.1, Botham: 8.0.33.0, Burgess: 8.0.26.1,
Dredge: 8.1.46.0, Jennings: 8.0.49.0.

Somerset innings

BC Rose	c and b Stevenson	23
PW Denning	b Robinson	53
*DB Close	run out	40
IT Botham	c and b Cooper	18
MJ Kitchen	not out	45
GI Burgess	not out	19
Extras (9 lb)		9
Total (4 wickets, 38 overs)		207

Fall of wickets: 1-47, 2-117, 3-121, 4-149

Did not bat: +DJS Taylor, D Breakwell, KF Jennings, CH Dredge,
HR Moseley.

Yorkshire bowling: Old: 8.1.22.0, Robinson: 8.0.38.1, Stevenson: 8.1.44.1,
Cope: 5.0.37.0, Cooper: 6.0.36.1, Carrick: 3.0.21.0.

Somerset won by 6 wickets

For Crying Out Loud

"Who's thingermejig?" said Gooch the blacksmith.

"You knows," said Farmer Emburey. "It's whatchermacallit. Him what is adored by millions and worshipped as the font of all bleeding knowledge … Him what brings solace to the sick, comfort to the weary, succour to the distraught and strength and eternal hope to the lovelorn."

"Colin Dredge!" said Miss Roebuck from the dog biscuit shop and collapsed instantly into a dead swoon.

The Brigadier in Season, Peter Tinniswood.

Come September 1978 Mervyn was on the brink of retirement, Closey had stood down as captain, replaced by Brian Rose to lead by his own admission "probably the scruffiest team ever in county cricket", and The Wurzels sang that "the rivers here are clear and clean in good old Somerset" on the car cassette player. I turned the music off. It was my flowing teenage tears that were at that moment clear and clean. I had witnessed a major slip-up. "Two bloody runs." I repeated the words over and over in my head. "We only needed a sodding draw."

"Two bloody runs," echoed my friend Clive, sat in the passenger seat. "What were Botham and Richards doing? Giving Essex catching practice? Dredge nearly did for us though."

"Yer, the Demon of Frome was nearly a ruddy hero. Top score of his life, I bet. But he owed us. It was his bowling to that Essex gnome Fletcher that cost us. And Budgie got nought. Nought!" In the Priory Road car park I repeatedly dabbed my eyes with a soggy hanky and stared at the steering wheel of my Austin 1100. It, too, had a damp air about itself having a few days before been dragged by tractor rope from the trout-laden River Barle. One lesson of being seventeen is not to leave the handbrake off when a car is pointing bonnet first and out of gear on a sloping riverbank when the driver's gone off dangling.

Another such life lesson was that supporting Somerset County Cricket Club would lead to heartbreak. Yet, I knew, for thousands, there was nothing but unstinting loyalty buoyed up by cider pints. The fact was Essex had simply got their own back.

The Gillette Cup semi-final at Taunton a fortnight earlier had seen Viv Richards hit a century. And in last ball mayhem, Essex had lost by virtue of having more wickets down in a match that was famously tied.

 I recalled my own state of sweated excitement as Somerset were moments from victory. "Last ball of the match," said the BBC commentator matter-of-factly into his microphone. "Three runs required. The last pair together. If Colin Dredge bowls another no ball they'll hang him here." The whole of Colin's enormous family were behind his arm. The Somerset songs 'Rosey's Army' and 'Cider Drinking' were hushed.

In an interview several years later Brian Rose relived his memory of that last ball to me. His face took on a haunted expression as he spoke. "I was actually praying at the time that the ball wouldn't come to me, and I think every other Somerset player was praying it wouldn't come to them either. I deposited nearly everybody, including the wicketkeeper Derek Taylor, on the boundary to stop the four or six obviously.

I can remember people behind me were so excited. The whole crowd was in a state of anxiety and that sort of rubbed off on me, really. The bloke behind me was virtually dying of heart failure. Then all I could see, all I remember, was John Lever having a swish at the ball. I didn't see the ball. I didn't pick the ball up for what seemed an eternity and could see Viv shouting and yelling at me to run. My legs felt like rubber. My chase was like slow motion to get to this ball. I was very lucky to pick it up at the first attempt."

What Brian omitted to say was that his throw was poo. However, Peter Roebuck in his book *Slices of Cricket* was too much of a gentleman to call it that. Merely that Brian "hurled the ball in first bounce, a yard off target." Derek collected it in a glove and dived full length at the wicket. Oh, wonderfulness.

But then the tear buckets were drawn from the emotion well of anticlimax.

But as Clive and I sat miserably in my car, Viv Richards, who a day earlier had hurled his Gillette Cup losers medal on the floor of the Lord's changing room, smashed his bat to smithereens. Two trophies gone in a weekend. Tragically surrendered. The only cups at Taunton came with saucers beneath them, and the wooden spoons of the County Championship had not a pot in which to stir. Yet every supporter knew Somerset's empty cabinet, silver-wise I mean, sorely mattered to that crop of players.

One year on and insurmountable joy meant the need for silver polish.

Twenty-two years ago I was the rural romantic supporting that underdog of fleeting flops and flickered lights, then twenty-one years ago that underdog came good. 'Rosey's Army' won both the Gillette Cup and John Player League in what was rather a grand weekend.

And having become the most successful skipper in Somerset's history, Rosey was granted a testimonial ... at Timsbury Cricket Club. Unfortunately, preparations for the match were severely hampered by some of the worst early season weather on record causing Timsbury's Chairman, Eric Nott, to make the glib comment that perhaps the club should hire "a whirlybird" to dry things out. Or was he just misheard saying "earlybird"? Yet somehow he had undoubtedly sowed the seed because, bless their cotton socks, somebody had a word in somebody's ear and with the backing of the club's sponsors, Bath Toyota, a hare-brained scheme got off the ground. To the 'dagga-dagga' sound of chopper blades Timsbury entered Cricket's history books as the first club in Britain to use a helicopter to dry out a pitch. On the morning after the match the *Daily Telegraph* carried the news to its avid readership both at home and across the world.

Anyway, with Somerset now having evolved into more of a golden retriever than a dachshund I simply remain the romantic. Gone were the days when a Somerset bowler might stick his tongue out at the umpire when an 'ell bee' – that's to say a leg before wicket – appeal was rejected. We were in the age of professionalism. Pinned to the walls at the bottom of the steps of Taunton's Andy Caddick Pavilion, and passed by batsmen on their way out to the middle, and back, are photos of Somerset successes. Among them are those that are now thirty years old, achieved by a Somerset team that included Viv Richards, Ian Botham and Joel Garner that had a habit of gleaning the glitzier one-day trophies. However, that team could never finish better than third in what the players and the purists regard as the greatest test, the Championship. And still a County Championship winning image remains unattained – a wait of a hundred and thirty-five years. But one must look optimistically to the future. Heavens, the County Championship must surely someday cease to be merely a chimera.

For those like my cricket-loving sons scraping runs and downing cider pints on village greens in the West Somerset League and who just hopped on the bandwagon of C&G and Twenty20 elation, palpable suffering had yet to test their strength of resolve. Indeed, with a bonus point here or a run there Somerset might even achieve more than the most cheerful optimist could ever hope for.

Sir Viv Richards v Barry Richards
Taunton, 1978

On the same page of the *Western Daily Press* of 18 September 1978 carrying news of Muhammad Ali regaining the World Boxing Association title after defeating Leon Spinks in the Louisiana Superdome was the headline "King Vivian rules" – a reference to the 'unofficial decider' for the world batting crown in which Sir Viv Richards did battle with the bat against South African Barry Richards.

The pair had faced 25 overs each before a crowd of 5,000 at Taunton. Billed as a 'unique challenge', it was the climax to Somerset wicket-keeper Derek Taylor's testimonial season. Neither batter was in good nick; Barry Richards had played only one innings – on a matting strip – since leaving Hampshire five weeks' earlier. Viv had not batted since smashing his favourite bat following Somerset's recent God-awful double defeat weekend, when the Gillette Cup and John Player League were lost on consecutive days.

The game saw the winner decided on runs per dismissal, so although Barry outscored Viv, his average was 38.2 per wicket against Viv's 68. The Antiguan won a solid silver trophy and prize money of £1,000 awarded by the Taunton Cider company. And with each six worth an extra tenner and every four a fiver, the pair earned an extra two hundred and thirty quid between them by way of eight sixes and thirty fours.

A Reason For Woe

SOMERSET v ESSEX

John Player League 1978
County Ground, Taunton on 3rd September 1978 (40-over match)
Somerset won the toss and decided to field

Umpires: WE Alley, DJ Halfyard

Essex innings

AW Lilley	c Denning	b Burgess	13
GA Gooch	c Burgess	b Botham	7
KS McEwan		b Moseley	2
*KWR Fletcher		not out	76
KR Pont		b Dredge	35
BR Hardie		b Botham	38
Extras (16 lb, 3 nb)			19
Total 5 wickets, innings closed, 40 overs)			190

Fall of wickets:1-16, 2-25, 3-29, 4-92, 5-190 (40 ov)

Did not bat: N Phillip, S Turner, RE East, +N Smith, JK Lever.

Somerset bowling: Botham: 8.0.38.2, Moseley: 8.0.20.1, Burgess: 8.0.20.1, Jennings: 8.0.38.0, Dredge: 8.0.55.1.

Somerset innings

*BC Rose		b Lever	9
PW Denning	c Smith	b Phillip	8
IVA Richards	c Hardie	b Gooch	26
PM Roebuck		b East	30
IT Botham	c McEwan	b Phillip	45
PA Slocombe		b Lever	20
GI Burgess	c and b Turner		0
KF Jennings		not out	14
CH Dredge		b Lever	14
+DJS Taylor		run out	4
HR Moseley		run out	0
Extras (2 b, 12 lb, 3 nb, 1 w)			18
Total (all out, 40 overs)			188

Fall of wickets: 1-18, 2-18, 3-69, 4-87, 5-139, 6-140, 7-157, 8-177, 9-185, 10-188 (40 ov)

Essex bowling: Lever: 8.0.38.3, Phillip: 8.0.35.2, Gooch: 8.0.31.1,
                     Turner: 8.0.32.1, East: 8.0.34.1.

Essex won by 2 runs.

THREE

Those Tingles Again

"No mind is much employed upon the present:
recollection and anticipation fill up almost all our moments."
Samuel Johnson (English Poet, Critic and Writer. 1709-1784).

"Time to wean them off the buttercups," said Bugsy, a moustached, limping, cider swigging, veteran of many seasons' cricket and rugby campaigning. The floral reference was towards the fluffy, yellow tennis balls that prettied the field of cricket coaching. 'Them' meant the young whippersnappers. 'To wean' meant that hard, leather-coated spheres were to be lobbed twenty-two yards towards those of tender years, a ritual toughening up process that sent mothers into apoplexies of anxiety.

Thoughts of whippersnapping bones caused a maternal scurrying to buy beloved offspring fibreglass and plastic body armour. Local sports shop cash tills rang, bucking recessional trends. Bugsy, for his part, was merely selflessly protecting the future of Wivey cricket. He could never entertain history repeating itself.

In 1857 Wivey, as Wiveliscombe is affably known, scored 8 all out against Milverton – an early nadir of achievement for my home town. Fingers crossed things had never got quite that bad since. Ophthalmologist William lbert Hancock F.R.C.S. had blazed the way, and in 1892 achieved the dizzying heights of playing in a single game for Somerset, making 0 and 7 against Surrey at the Oval. It was sorry reading for the eyes of our prominent Guy's hospital's cricketer, and the cold light of day made William decide to stick to rugby union where he and six of his ten brothers would represent the county more successfully.

Yet, although batting averages might have read like shoe-sizes, at least the local bowling department was to become more dependable, attaining its zenith in 1950.

During one fortnight that season local born lad Jack Conibere played four consecutive first-class games for Somerset, albeit on a trial basis. By the end of the second week his first-class cricket career as a left-arm fast-medium pacer was abruptly terminated. Ah well, no one really fretted. Jack was probably a better player running about in the mud with a big oval ball, a county star. Hereabouts that counted for a lot more. And this being rugby country, I regret to say, a few still think of cricket as means of merely passing away the time when leaves coat the trees.

Anyway, at least Jack had tried his best with the little hard ball. Mind you, things had gone tickety-boo in the first of his Somerset outings – four Warwickshire first innings wickets for 66 runs at Edgbaston. Indeed, with the help of Bertie Buse and Maurice Tremlett, Jack had half the side out for 47. Not bad for starters. And come the Bears second innings he took two more. The problem was he only managed to snaffle one more wicket in the three games that followed.

Jack's zealous exploits aside, praise for Wivey's general bowling achievements should be lavished upon Roger Masters, the aptly named Kingsmead schoolteacher who would generously place 6d from his own pocket on the middle stump in the lunch break nets to induce accuracy of committed pupils. Both sweet money and matches became won simultaneously, although Wivey's fortunes demised again in the years following Roger's retirement. But all this was before my day.

Wivey is a rarity – a club without a clubhouse, that instead makes do with the bowels of the singularly arcane rugby stand. Now with the massing of the primroses and shrinking violets it was time to put away the rugby posts and to sluice down the muddied and bloodied rugby changing rooms in preparation for the men who reckoned on playing games in laundered whites. And a key would need to be sought for the 'store cupboard'. Inside this hole of spiders and mice was the old school easel, the time-worn, nail studded, scoreboard, and the craftsman made plates of tin numbers that along with sets of stumps and a motley array of club kit would be dragged out into the daylight of spring. And at home, my whites, scrunched, fetid, within the below stairs cubbyhole, were in need of airing.

Beyond the garden gate, and across the county of Somerset, from Dulverton in the west to Temple Cloud in the east, heavy rollers squashed flat the rich tilth of molehills, mounds that over the forthcoming months would further benefit from frequent end-of-bat-tap-gardening.

For visitors to actually find the pitches would again be a match day compli-
cation. Adding "as the crow flies" to guesstimated distances without newfangled 'sat navs' was always advisable before setting out for away games that
lay down unfamiliar tracks. A problem exacerbated by crossroads, hedges, a
lack of signposts, and crops such as sweet corn or tall elephant grass, that
create a rural maze disorientating even the local navigator in search of the
hidden qualities of say the postage-stamp-sized pitch at Roadwater's Valiant
Beer Garden, where batting averages for the sober-headed would often take
an upturn.

Given that Roadwater held certain magnetism, other grounds also had their
attractions. In Ashbrittle, the 'Hillbillies', that's to say the gaggle of the four
talented cricketing Hill brothers, though one, a dead ringer for Rodney out of
the BBC's *Only Fools and Horses* was deemed 'too lazy' to play for Somerset,
would no doubt be intending to illustrate that unity continued to be strength,
and dependable as the village's 3000 year old yew tree.

Near the foot of Bleadon Hill, known locally as "Bleedin' 'Ell", possibly
because of the past bloodbath of a battle there between Saxons and Vikings,
Sam Trego, the older brother of Somerset's Peter, would be captaining Uphill
Castle for another season of sibling rivalry. And under the shadow of another
hill, Ham Hill, a fellow with the inspiring surname of Nelson would, if
history repeated itself, be specialising in first aid upon himself at West and
Middle Chinnock.

While elsewhere, and carrying over from last season when their wicket-
keeper's gloves were described as "bed pans", the argument over a small
matter of interpretation would probably still be raging in Baltonsborough.
The club's badge of crossed swords over a set of stumps seemed singularly
appropriate.

And whereas folk in Beckington could wallow in the nostalgia of their club
being one of the oldest clubs in the country following discovery of docu-
mentation referring to 1884 as the "re forming of the village cricket club", a
chimney sweep in Dunster, a happy-go-lucky club less than a decade old,
would be wallowing in worry.

Lou would already have a strong nylon net suspended over his boundary
edge garden's prize carp pond. Nominally the net was there as a deterrent
against the stab of herons, but it was also there to minimise sudden headaches
occurring to his beloved fish, many much older than the Exmoor village club,
from the landing of cricket balls thwacked from Dollons Meadow.

Up on Exmoor, on a farm in the shadow of Dunkery Beacon, Polly the border collie sheepdog would be limbering up for her excited ball pursuits as Wootton Courtenay's adopted third man by chasing a spring chicken or two.

And Whitchurch still had a bone to pick with Neil should they catch up with him, he having shifted his playing allegiance from Fitzhead to Wellington. The lad had hit a skier causing two Whitchurch fielders to arrive from opposite direction in an attempt to make the catch only to be both thwarted by Neil's shout of "Mine!" allowing the ball to drop harmlessly between them.

In Taunton, 'Shadows' gathered. And the county's professionals began to assemble again at Starbucks. To me this was unsurprising as rumour had it that the menu for the Somerset team's 7.30 am breakfast was baked fish – salmon or halibut – accompanied by raw broccoli and raw carrots. Mind you, 'The Great Alfonso', deferred to a roll-up with his swig of black coffee.

Among the coffeehouse melee of these modern adverts for the Cider County was new arrival Nick Compton, grandson of Dennis Compton. Whereas James Hildreth would be conservative with an americano, Nick would order a mug of "milky froth with chocolate sprinkles".

There too would be Max Waller, ex Millfield School captain and legbreak bowler to whom no batsman had as yet been reduced to crutches. "Strawberries and Cream frappuccino," Max would order until an exasperated young barista with big hair, who I have to admit was my youngest son, Wivey's wicky and number 5 bat, audaciously told his elder and better to "Man up".

There was a renewed sense of optimism in the wind, as well the occasional snow flurry. Excitable sorts began to declare James Hildreth as the next Bradman.

With the wonderfulness of promotion the season before, Wivey, could look forward to life in Division 1 of the West Somerset League and rubbing noses with the elites of the likes of Ashbrittle, Brompton Ralph and Bridgetown. Other teams played in the Shrubbery which was nowt to do with hedges, greenery and creepy-crawlies, but was the rather Pythonesque name adopted by reasons of sponsorship for the Somerset League.

"Sleep when you're dead, play cricket while you're awake" are the words of advice eagerly followed from Taunton's County Ground to the many a twenty–two yards treasured down a country lane.

*

Down my lane where dandelion clocks caught by the wind disintegrated into annoying parachutes Peckal the tame hen blackbird had taken it upon herself to nest lay her eggs in the hydrangea petiolaris that climbed with profusion over my warped blue front door. The browned-off bird eyed her mate anxiously as with a skip in my step I played a cover drive with the year's first stick of rhubarb and burst forth into song in false accented Zummerset:

> That bird'll be the death of me,
> he's prayin' on me mind!
> If I chase him long enough,
> I'll get 'en by and by,
> And celebrate me vict'ry
> wit a girt big blackbird pie!
> Where be it Blackbird to?
> I know where he be,
> He be up yon Wurzel tree,
> And I be after he!

The song had been sung in the off-season somewhere up in India's north, Hyderabad I think, where Somerset's cricketers had beaten Deccan Chargers in a T20 game and had sung lustily about that blackbird in a Wurzel tree and a great big stick to knock him down. It was, by all accounts, the happiest moment of captain Justin Langer's illustrious eighteen season first class career. Towards the end of it, at Worcester in July 2009, he had become the highest-scoring Australian batsman in first-class cricket when he overhauled Sir Donald Bradman's career total of 28,067 runs going past the milestone with a cover drive for four off fellow Australian Matt Mason.

God bless Adge Cutler, I thought. May God bless Wivey. But most of all, God bless Somerset. I offered a silent prayer that the new season might bring professional honours, perhaps, at a very shot, even the holy grail of the Championship. Though tedious to relate, Somerset remained the only first class county other than Northamptonshire never to won the blessed thing. And they had both had over a hundred goes at it. However, Justin Langer's tenure as a disciplinarian toughie of a county skipper couldn't be said to have ended fruitlessly at the previous season's close.

A waistline-slimming exercise regime seemed to appal some players. It had been much too tough for his predecessor, the rotund Ian Blackwell known to some of his mates as 'Le Donk' or 'Donkey' and to others as 'Blackdog'. After finding himself in the doghouse and unable to see eye to eye, and also perhaps aware that Justin was something of a martial arts expert, Le Donk had headed for black pudding breakfasts in the old Viking lands of Dunholm, that's to say, Durham.

"Making this cricketing decision has been the hardest thing I've ever had to do," he commented, before treading the path previously taken by Sir Beefy, and losing ten kilograms in the process. However, Le Donk probably allowed himself a smile at the *Guardian* comment: "In the time that Langer takes to study the ingredients on a low-fat yoghurt, Blackwell could down a pork pie and a couple of pints of real ale."

I for one, amidst other Somerset fans, rather missed chanting "Who ate up all the pies?" or "C'mon Blackie give us a wave" from Taunton's defunct rickety river stand whose ghost sat in the shadow of shady new apartments. And as for Justin, folk in the stands just shrug when asked how he got the name Alfie. And most just look plain baffled when told his other alias is BNG, an acronym for Brown Nosed Gnome.

I recently put this to a thirty-something fellow passenger, one wearing a 'WACA Warriors' T-shirt, florescent three quarter lengths, and flip-flops, reading a sports mag, on the Fremantle to Perth commuter train, thinking he must know any answers posed about Western Australia's most famous of sons. "Mate," he said, "to us he's just Langer. Ain't Alfie a Pom bloke on your Eastenders?" "Be blessed," I said. "Justin's also been called 'Australia's Samuel Pepys'."

The T-shirt looked at me for signs of madness. Then I added that Justin apparently writes he's "the luckiest person in the world" into his journal at the end of every day. So I knew not to mention subjective appraisal wasn't the only the only thing that inspired Justin. When signing a copy of his book *Seeing the Sunrise* for some Christian minister or other, Justin scribbled, at the good man's request, a Bible verse of Justin's own choosing. "God doesn't give us the spirit of fear, but of love, strength, and a sound mind (2 Timothy 1:7)" is reportedly what he penned.

Oh Lordy, as fate would have it, fingers-crossed, Banger 'Mad Fish' Trescothick's tenure as captain of Somerset was about to begin. Yes, 'Mad Fish' is his nickname along with that of 'Banger', and 'Fish' is plainly marker-penned for all to see on the peak of his faded, sweat stained, duck-billed limited overs cap.

But why the 'mad' bit? Well, blame Guy Ritchie's 2000 film *Snatch* and Marcus's 'mates' in the dressing room. In the movie there is a character that clearly goes potty and ends up shooting himself. The Somerset lads all think that was the way he has been living for a few years, Marcus confided to a Eurosport reporter. However, I'm not going to be the one to tell Marcus that he needs to reach again for the marker pen. My 'googling' discovered the character to be called 'Mad Fist Willy' not 'Mad Fish'.

Justin and Marcus seemed a bit like chalk and cheese, or let's say a latte and a skinny grande vanilla macciato. However, everyone could only wish Marcus luck. He had come a long way since 1995 when the then *Independent* correspondent Derek Pringle was on hand at Taunton to report on Somerset playing Richie Richardson's touring West Indies side. The unfortunate Pringle is often remembered for his bizarre warm-up routine before coming on to bowl that involved him lying on his back and apparently wrestling with an invisible octopus, and later being caught picking his nose on camera in a foreign press box, and admiring the nasal discovery upon his fingernail. What happened next? Well, this was a question asked on BBC's *Question of Sport.* The right answer was he gobbled the little treasure up. Of course he did. And this being the man who picked The Soft Boys track *I Wanna Destroy You* for Rough Trade Records 30th Anniversary Compilation album.

At Taunton Derek proved his perceptive qualities in a more orthodox manner by writing: "Trescothick, not yet 19, has a more orthodox method (than Mark Lathwell), though he too needs to work on knowing where his off-stump is. Against the predicted short stuff, he looked admirably solid. However, as soon as Benjamin pitched up, the young left-hander edged behind, opening the face of his bat as the ball left him off the pitch." Marcus has kept the open-face habit, but I relied on him not being tempted too often. Hope sprang eternal.

Like me, friends, too, admitted to having the pre-season tingles and seemed to be of similar mind of hopefulness whichever village team claimed their loyalties. And all would be listening in as they created things of beauty, be it Phil the carpenter building a rowing boat in his barn loft when not scoring for Lydeard St Lawrence, or Mooseman creating a sculpture in his secret woodland artist studio and declaring mercenary status.

Even Bessbo my aged cat would seem to leave off her voling-moling in the allotment asparagus bed to curl up beside me, and the laptop. With her ear to the internet commentaries she would open an eye should a reporter from BBC Warwickshire or BBC Essex erroneously cite the Mendips as being visible behind Taunton's Sir Ian Botham and Marcus Trescothick stands instead of the Quantocks.

*

On the walls of the 'Bearin' Up', the affectionate name for Wivey's *Bear Inn*, old posters for "Hitty, Hitty Bang Bang" vied for space with fresher affairs declaring "Danger – Batsmen at Work". Newfangled Twenty-20 cricket that allowed sane chaps to don the likes of fluffy polyester Friesian cow suits and tinkle bells to accompany the bim-boms of St Mary Magdelene had got the rapt attention of the phlegmatic if not the traditionalist.

I joined a couple of such stoics, Richard and his grown-up son Ian bibbling pints of Tawny ale at a table in a dimly lit pub corner. Grey bearded Richard was able to boast of having dusted down his library of cricket books so that they were spring-cleaned with new season freshness.

Retired as a sales rep selling animal feedstuffs to Exmoor farmers, Richard was a Londoner who liked to describe himself as "a countryman from the City". Rather than support Middlesex or Surrey he had decided to follow Somerset with zealous fervour ever since the 1970s when in the days of the John Player League a wag sat beside him shouted to a wayward bowling Bob Clapp, "Lad, you're hogging three lanes, trying keeping to the middle one!"

"Reminds me a little of Walter Darby," I said. "He was a great cricketer. Played for Winsford and was a bit of a guddler. When tight as a tick he used to say, 'I see three balls and I always hit the middle un'". Actually, Walter became a legend when Winsford played Porlock away. He was so pickled that his team mates drove off without him. So, bless him, he ran all way to Porlock, almost eleven miles as the crow flies up and down across Exmoor heather, through many a gorse bush, and around many a hawthorn tree, bullock, sheep and pony, batted and won the match himself.

The greatest legend to Richard though was Joel 'Big Bird' Garner who he often observed taking "five minutes" to uncurl his six foot nine inch frame from behind the wheel of his cramped little car to put in fuel at the forecourt pumps of Wivey's Jones's Garage. How could Richard not support Somerset out of sympathy?

A man of many hats, as opposed to caps, for his roles in the local community, Richard now felt connected to the county side. That son of a Scotswoman, Craig Kieswetter, had opened Wivey church fête the year before. For 'Kieso' to agree to do the honour was down to Richard's persuasive nature after witnessing a singularly spectacular demolition of the Gloucestershire bowling attack. And the 'countryman from the City' had swelled with pride when, several months after the feted occasion, Kieso had lowered down the black tinted window of his newly acquired lowered suspension black Range Rover to say "Hi, Richard", outside Sainsbury's.

"Yep, he's a nice guy," I said, and a look of surprise crossed Richard' face when I mentioned that my son Felix was on Kieso's Facebook list of friends. With the church fête soon to be looming again, he was quick to ask whether Felix was a friend to any other Somerset player. Having been satisfied that I would inquire, Richard cogitated on the summer ahead with Ian, reappointed captain of Fitz-head, a team whose exponential curve of success hadn't had any significant surges since their nadir of 1959 when Wellington skittled them for 19.

Prematurely grey himself, Ian led a team who hadn't won a match in the Shrubbery for a year. Several players were green, team morale was low, talent was woefully lacking, and Ian seemed resigned to the possibility of team temper tantrums. Some players in the past though, he admitted, had gone a little too far. One distraught fellow, his pride injured by being given out ell bee, 'lamped' the umpire and then went home and shot himself. Either that or he hanged himself. Ian couldn't quite remember which.

I looked into my beer glass, discomforted. Sadly I knew cricketing suicide touched all levels of play. According to David Frith's research in *Silence of the Heart*, of the 339 England Test cricketers who had died by July 2000, 1.77 per cent were suicides. Tragically among them was Harold Gimblett. Though G Morehouse described him playing the game "vividly, sturdily, and above all gallantly", he was also the man David Foot described as the "tormented genius of cricket".

Indeed, in 1978, two years before he died, Harold called up David and asked him for help to write a book. "The mental battles for me have been enormous," he said, "and maybe it would be a good idea to put it on record." Harold spoke into a tape recorder.

Three decades after Gimblett's death, clinical depression is better understood. Better medication has been developed to control it, and even if it is still a mystery to the lay person, the medical bumpf on it is extensive mercifully to Marcus Trescothick's benefit.

The rule for autobiographies was laid down by George Orwell: an autobiography is only to be trusted when it reveals something disgraceful. David Foot's biography of Harold Gimblett and Marcus Trescothick's autobiography *Coming Back to Me* stand out both for speaking the truth and revealing something "disgraceful". But never was the so-called disgraceful revealed with more grace than it was in these books. The illness that dare not speak its name – mental illness – is discussed with an openness that is heroic.

To many Harold was the greatest batsman Somerset's ever produced. His century in 63 minutes against Essex at Frome's Agricultural Showground in 1935, his first county match was straight out of Boys' Own. There he was, having been rejected by Somerset after Taunton trials, hitchhiking to Frome as a last minute replacement and going in at number 8 having borrowed the bat of the man said to be the best poacher in Somerset, Arthur Wellard. Harold's innings made him, at 20, the most famous cricketer in the country and won him the Walter Lawrence Trophy.

Unsurprisingly, the suicide figures are even higher in that country of hot red dust, Australia. They have to beat us at everything, don't they? And, for South Africa the numbers are astonishing, 4.12 per cent.

Uniquely among team games, cricket cruelly highlights the temperament, skill and perseverance of the individual. The cricketer has no hiding place. The scorecard reveals to the world – not just to team-mates but to friends, relatives, lovers and most of all himself.

And from my own experience, failing to get hands on a dolly catch as I back-peddled faster and faster up Timberscombe's severely sloping pitch before toppling over like a Falkland's penguin radiated a sense of reproach from Bugsy, bowling dibbly-dobblies, and my fellow Wivey 2nds team-mates. Their collective "Way to go Tiger!" made me wish for instant oblivion, and the incident continued to haunt me several seasons on. But while chatting to Ian and Richard I kept all this to myself. Who was I to put a damper on convivial banter?

I merely picked up on the Fizhead affair and offered to Ian that adverse ell bee decisions can affect the good humour of anyone, even the most lauded individual For example Lancashire members ducked for cover as Sir Vivian Richards' bat flew in a shower of glass splinters through the plate glass dressing room window of Old Trafford pavilion, known then as the 'Pit of Hate'. An event for which Somerset later issued a tongue in cheek apology saying that the bat "had bounced off the floor".

And then, of course, there was Justin Langer's deed of destruction. The dour Aussie smashed a very large, very old wicker dressing room laundry basket to smithereens with his bat. He redressed the matter by giving money from his wallet to his wife Sue to go and try to buy a replacement.

"Yes, but at Fitzhead we don't harm inanimate objects, we tend to do harm to ourselves," Ian responded. And with undisguised embarrassment he related the goings-on that had happened at Taunton St Andrew's. There, Fitzhead's Australian wicketkeeper clad in a protective helmet with a titanium grille had a heated dispute over a missed catching opportunity with first slip. Things boiled over into full-on fisticuffs. It was the proverbial pitch battle. As the pair rained blows at the head of each other, Ian, with a captain's responsibility, tried unsuccessfully to separate the antagonists. The rest of the team just stood wincing at and admiring the impromptu entertainment. Needless to say, Ian concluded, the helmeted Aussie eventually won.

However, a new season beckoned. Perhaps things might improve for the better. "Well, there's always hope," said Ian into his pint glass, almost dreading the imminent arrival of Huish and Langport.

I dream of many a glorious drive,
I feel the cut that goes for five,
I hear the crowd's applauding roar
That follows oft a hook for four.

EBV Christian.

F O U R

From Whence The Hurt Came

*"Some old stories I have heard of cricket matches, which I own, however,
to be so strange and incredible that, if I had not received them from
eye-witnesses, I could never have yielded to them any belief."*

The Gentleman's Magazine, September 1743.

Phil the Boat didn't quite fit *Guardian* writer David Foot's description of a Somerset man. He didn't have a rosy face. Neither did he speak slowly, caressing and rolling his 'rs' with a rural relish. Nor did his eyes sparkle with an engaging cunning. Phil's eyes had just shone with pure undisguised excitement as he urbanely scratched his arse. It hadn't taken much persuasion for him to desert his station of scorebook and biro for a chance of actually playing for Lydeard St Lawrence seconds, a team lacking numbers on that bivvering day of woolly-pullies at season's start on a pitch, offering uneven bounce, recovered from the earth works of moles.

By his own admission Phil, gangly, gentle, and bookish, had as much chance of hitting a hurtling cricket ball with his ancient stick of willow as a flying clay pigeon with a 12 bore. Nor was he any Brian Close, whose bloody-minded doggedness, bald pate, and brick shithouse-sized frame could withstand any flurry of potential bone-breaking leather cherries.

Phil saw himself more as being from the grey-haired, steel rimmed glasses school of bravery that was less Peter Roebuck, recently named as opener in the team of best un-capped England players of all time, and more David Steele, the Northants batsman the *Sun's* Clive Taylor described in the 1970s as "The bank clerk who went to war". Indeed he did, his head protected by only a cap, first against Lilley and Thompson and then against Roberts and Holding et al. Naturally David became a national hero for his pains in an England career that lasted only eight matches and little more than a year.

And there was no wearing of a helmet with a grille for Phil. He had no wish to blink at the world as if he was a budgie in a cage. A faded 'Steele-like' cap sufficed to shade a weak spring sun from his eyes.

Hero of the West Somerset variety, he wandered out to face Milverton's raw and ambitious sapling fast bowler. The youth exhibited no finesse in his thought process, like for instance, pitching the new ball up in hope of some swing, then later, and only later, as the sphere became worn of bowling short, to make the batter duck and sway. No, this young gun arched his back with the simple philosophy of launch to kill.

Phil meanwhile intended to rely on a firm, long-striding forward stroke as he took his 'middle' guard. Regretfully, whereas Grey David was rewarded with 1,756 lamb chops from a butcher for every run he scored in his benefit season, Phil just got one in the chops the first ball he received.

After a moment or two of concentrated scrutiny the umpire's decision to the sapling's squawk of "HOWZAT!" was: "You've 'it 'im on the 'ead, lad."

For the uninitiated there are two types of injury. Firstly, there are those that generate hysterics of laughter such as an umpire pulling his gluteus maximus taking evasive action, a batter getting pinged in 'the box' or, best of all, Wivey's Gary badly winding himself taking a corker of a diving catch at slip.

Gary would be the first to admit that he's not the slimmest of fellows and trying to fly horizontally has consequences. If Glamorgan's South Australian star Mark Cosgrove is rotund, then Gary is positively spherical, more of a clog than a slipper. His effusive belly-flopping dives are seismic. While his breathy exhalation on landing resembles the popping of an inflated lilo, his pursuant groans are like the creaking of a rusty-hinged barn door. So side splittingly funny it is to behold that opposition batters have become known to try and actually snick the ball in Gary's direction, then stand back and admire the spectacle.

On the other hand, there are those cringeworthy on field nasties that produce nausea in the pits of tummies. Like for example in those of folk that witnessed the unfortunate incident involving the Marquis de Taunton, as 'Long John' Francis has become called due to him running a Taunton marquee company. He was hit on the temple by Matt Wood's fizzing tracer of a throw-in against the Scottish Saltires in 2005. Insult in that game was added to injury as ergo the cidermen had to bat one short and slumped to a 15 run defeat.

At least Long John lived, as did Viv Richards, who after being hit on the temple by a bouncer from the asthmatic Aussie Rodney Hogg, the man that famously complimented the Queen on her legs, dispatched the next ball into the twelfth row at square leg.

Jasper Vinall wasn't so fortunate. In 1624, in the days before bats became big and uniform in shape, an Edward Tye playing 'crickett' with 'the husband-men of West Hoathly' hit the ball in the air and then endeavoured, 'for his greater advantage' to hit it again as it plummeted. Jasper, however, 'arrived suddenly behind his back' and was clouted by Edward's 'bacillus', that's to say a smallish stick probably resembling a rounders baton. Instantaneously Jasper became cricket's first fatality, one an inquest deemed 'unwitting' accident.

Thankfully, Phil's mishap ranked alongside Long John's. After the yelp came a lot of blood, soul loss, and a visit to A & E.

A week or so later, Phil, resplendent with blue bruised fizzog, received a large blow up of a photograph in the post from a friend who by chance had snapped the moment of impact. He showed it to me.

"Look, you can see the martins swooping, gathering the seed heads of the rye grass," said Phil jabbing a finger at the tiny boomerangs of birds caught on camera flying behind his pads.

"Daft apeth," I replied as one that once wore a yellow motorcycle helmet to face a bowler with a penchant for removing metal caps from beer bottles with his teeth. " In this world of ducking and diving you're a daft bloody apeth."

"I'm sure cricket balls get harder," Phil quipped sagely, at last allowing himself a grimace, and me thinking, "But for the grace of God".

I suppose he was right about the balls, but tracing the evolution, like with bats, lends itself to guesswork.

There was a time when a leather sphere, four inches in diameter, was stuffed with boiled quills. Surely a blow from such a ball couldn't have done too much damage. However, quarrymen and miners on the Mendips as well as Exmoor shepherds bucked the trend by using a club to larrup a stone instead of a ball. That though was in the seventeenth century when the game enjoyed by Somerset's farm labourers and miners was known as 'stow-ball' rather than 'crickets' and apparently played with two bats, a bowler and fieldsmen; well, so says the *Oxford English Dictionary*. And indeed, Bicknoller-born Harold Gimblett had his own "Roaring Twenties" variant.

He used to play for hours, a tree at his Blakes Farm home as a wicket, in those formative years before he played for Watchet, let alone Somerset. His elder brothers Lewis and Dennis would bowl stones at him just to see how far he could wallop them.

The word 'stow' was dialect for the lower part of a tree, or its remaining stump. It was also the name given to a frame used to support crawling tunnels in the North Somerset lead mines that provided another possibility for the wicket. It's only due to an inky penned memo on a handkerchief now owned by the MCC that it's decreed that a wicket should be 22 inches high.

John Aubrey, the famous anthropologist, actually recorded watching stow-ball being played up the road in north Wiltshire being played in the evenings back in 1686. He noted that men used "withy staves" to wallop the ball and that their owners had carefully shaped themselves, and that when any boy reached the age of eight he was given two staves by his father. By all accounts the staves were shaped similar to field hockey sticks.

At this point one mustn't forget the Gillmeister Theory that cricket was invented in Belgium, conceived by Herr Heiner Gillmeister, a linguist from Germany's University of Bonn. He was of the opinion that it was Flemish weavers who first brought the game of cricket to England and played it close to where they looked after their sheep, using shepherd's crooks as bats using a 'ball' made from a sheep's bladder possibly filled with wool. But for mention of the odd stone on Exmoor, Phil's evolutionary conjecture was holding up well.

Added to this, in Middle Dutch, the language of medieval Flanders, "krick(e)" meant a stick, although in Olde English, "cricc" or "cryce" meant a crutch or staff. However, Flemish weavers did indeed settle in Somerset from the fourteenth century onwards. They were the forebears of many a rebel who fought for the Taunton 'crowned' king of England, James Scott Duke of Monmouth, at the gory Battle of Sedgemoor in the summer of 1685 when games of cricket weren't really on the agenda.

What we do know is that, initially, it seems the local population resisted the temptation to play the game. A poem called *The Image of Ipocrisie* written in 1533 attributed to John Skelton reads:

> O lodre of Ipocrites,
> Nowe shut vpp your wickettes,

And clappe to your clickettes!
A! Farewell, kings of crekettes!

Thankfully, over time Somerset folk saw sense. At least they had done so when a Covent Garden barber's son, the landscape artist Joseph Mallord William Turner visited Wells in the summer of 1791 during his teenage years while holidaying with family relations who lived in Bristol.

Now, in the Lady Lever Art Gallery way up north at Port Sunlight, a place built on the profits of washing powder, hangs a watercolour of Wells Cathedral painted by young JMW No sketches he made on the spot appear to have survived and the picture was a studio based affair after Turner had returned to London, perhaps as much as four years after his West Country visit. Yet, pictured outside the cathedral's main entrance are, without a shadow of doubt, a motley group of blokes playing cricket with curved bats and two stumps. Was this artistic licence by the venerable painter? By following Phil the Boat's train of thought, one could only fear for the stained glass if there was an early version of a Woods, Gimblett, Botham, Richards, or even a Trego or Buttler among them.

And if there had been a Wells game, what had actually inspired it? Well, all that can be said is that the earliest confirmed reference to cricket in Somerset is a match on the 13 July 1751 that was played in memory of the late Frederick, Prince of Wales, a noted patron of the sport.

"Dad, did you know cricket was invented by the Chinese?" queried my son Felix, all big hair, designer wear and a-buzz, bursting through our warped blue front door on his return from a day's college education. "And 'popping crease' came from a hole which a fielder had to pop the ball in before the batsman made his ground by jabbing his bat's butt end into the hole first. Logical, innit?"

"Really?" I replied nonplussed. "How interesting." Theories never ceased as to the origins of my addiction.

*

No game was ever yet worth a rap,
For a rational man to play,
Into which no accident, no mishap,
Could possibly find its way.

Adam Lindsay Gordon (Australian poet, 1833–1870).

FIVE

Knowing One's Bats

Strange fascination of a wooden bat!
Weird magic hidden in a leathern ball!

Strange fascinations these; in serried ranks
We see men sit throughout the livelong day
Content! Strange fascinations, that do build
A very world of fellowship, for those
That play. Fools laugh, they cannot understand;
Are we fools too?

DLA Jephson (1871-1926).

"Cricket is the greatest thing that God created on earth. Certainly greater than sex, although sex isn't too bad either." So wrote the husband of actress Vivian Merchant, Harold Pinter, the Jewish tailor's son who blossomed into the famous English playwright enjoying affairs with Joan Bakewell and Lady Antonia Fraser. Vivian turned to alcoholism and an early grave. Although one may wonder at God's penchant for leather and willow, it could be doubted that, in retrospect, the good scribe quite got his priorities right.

Indeed, some memories, those that have the tendency to send one pale, are hard to shift. Here, I too, can speak from experience…

"Four!"

The excited voice of my four-year-old son Felix had drifted through my open study window.

"Six!"

Bless, I thought.

"Seven!"

I frowned.

Then a coarse woman's voice turned the air blue. "Ya little buggers! Oi'm goin' ta chop em inta foyarwood! Oi'll teach ya for hittin' crabbies inta me 'ome!"

Firewood? I had deciphered the word. Oh gawd. There was a danger of history repeating itself, and I couldn't let it happen.

To be fair the crab apple thing was my fault, a discovered joy passed on. When I was grasshopper high, my grandpapa Harold gave me a present of a grey, mildew mottled canvas bag with worn leather handles. "I hope you can have fun with this," he said with a smile full of good intention before chuckling, "And don't go hogging the bowling like Collins the sprog," a ribald reference to a thirteen year public school boy of Clifton College who over several late afternoons in 1899 must really have begun to irritate.

By the time the umpiring housemasters of a junior house match went to put their feet up young Arthur Collins, after winning the toss and opening the batting, had amassed an unbeaten 628 in seven hours at the crease out of 836 for Clark's House. In so doing he broke the world record for the highest innings. The opposition, North House, capitulated with a token riposte. Possibly due to the need to get the hell off the pitch and finish pressing and overdue homework, or just to get on with life, they scored a measly 148 over their two innings and became losers by a stonking 688 runs. Some, the mere mortals suffering from the lonely tedium of the outfielder, may even have thought to have given up cricket altogether and try fishing instead.

Any supercilious smile the sprog may have had after his batting performance would no doubt have widened as he returned bowling figures of 11 for 63.

Being a man of the cloth Grandpapa Harold obviously thought the sprog unchristian in inflicting such excessive suffering on fellow creatures. Basically he was a romantic, one for the poetic, though preferring Thomas Moult to William Shakespeare or John Keats.

He would lean on a wide, iron hinged wooden gate that spanned the gap in bluebell and stitchwort-crammed hedge banks watching an afternoon's village cricket match as I stood on the second plank up, peering over, too. And he would softly recite *The Names* accompanied by birdsong, insect hum, the frequent click of willow hitting leather and shouts from the field of "Oh, for Heaven's sake".

"There's music in the names I used to know,
And magic when I heard them long ago.
'Is Tyldesly batting?' Ah, the wonder still!
… The school clock crawled, but cricket thoughts would fill
The last slow lesson-hour deliciously.
(Drone on, O teacher: you can't trouble me.)

'Kent will be out by now.'… (Well, if you choose
To keep us here while cricket's in the air,
You must expect our minds to wander loose
Along the roads to Leicester, Lord's and Leeds,
Old Trafford and the Oval, and the Taunton meads…)

And then at last, we'd raid the laneway where
A man might pass, perchance, with latest news,
Grey-grown and grave, yet he would smile to hear
Our thirsty questions as we crowded near,
Greedily from the quenching page we'd drink –
How its white sun-glare made our young eyes wink!
'Yes, Tyldesley's batting still. He's ninety-four.
Barlow and Mold play well. Notts win once more.
Glo'ster (with Grace) have lost to Somerset -
Easy: ten wickets: Woods and Palariat…'"

By looking inside Grandpapa Harold's bag I saw that he had passed his own youth on to me. There was a pair of 'old school' pads of negligible utility constructed of wadding and cane, an equally useless pair of manky cotton gloves on the backs and fingers of which were perished rubber spikes, and my first full size cricket bat. There were suspicious woodwormy holes in the splice, and it came with strong whiff of linseed oil. There were no logos, no makers' names – just a lump of dark wood with crack in the toe-end bound with tender loving care with what had become timeworn twine.

But let it be said, this was a bat from Jesus. Well, Jesus College, Cambridge, at any rate. Grandpapa had collared the second-hand timber artefact during his student days at the turn of the twentieth century after it had been begrudgingly left behind by its original owner who had occupied Harold's room a couple of years before him.

"It had belonged to a chap by the name of Woods. Turned out to be a fine cricketer, one of the 'Names'," Grandpapa related to me. "Certainly he was a better sportsman than a scholar. All he wrote on his exam paper was 'Dam'. The dear fellow couldn't spell even the simplest word of blasphemy. By all accounts he was whacking something unmentionable around the quad when the bat was confiscated by old Solomon the college porter who later exchanged it with me for a jar of plum chutney."

As Grandpapa told me to enjoy the bat he also advised that I had better use it to hit tennis balls rather than those of the leather, hurtful variety. And for a time tennis balls it was until I discovered the joys of thumping crab apples for six.

Then came an invitation to play in a match, albeit not a particularly serious one. With youthful recklessness I relied on playing with the dodgy bat. Silly me. The blade shattered into pieces, detaching itself from the handle to the first tentative defensive prod offered to a hard ball, which to be fair, was bowled at what I considered to be considerable speed.

Sometime after the relic had become winter fire kindling I learned too late that the bat was a sanctified relic far better off in the gloom of Taunton's cricket museum, racked in the company of bats of previously significant ownership. Perhaps even near the one standing beside a notice ordering "Do Not Touch", the bat of Somerset's God Almighty, the man who said "It's always good beating the Australians – and it's even better to beat them out there. But the Ashes are just one thing. Ask me for the biggest highlight when I'm lying on my deathbed – then I'll tell you." On loan by Tom Higgins, having been handed down and then handed down again, Sir Ian Botham's bat, wielded in the famous 1981 Ashes series, ended up being used by an eleven year old in a garden, and likely as not splattered the odd windfall.

The student to whom my relic had first belonged was Australian-born SMJ Woods, revered by many simply as Sammy. His career began soon after Somerset began to take cricket seriously, at least to the extent of batsmen not skipping to the wicket wearing a straw hat and carrying an ice cream along with a bat. Sammy, county captain, and fearsome batsman and bowler, during his nineteen years at Somerset that ended in 1910, scored 12,637 runs and took 556 wickets at an average of 24.1. He was also a womaniser, a hider of cider bottles in hedgerows and was photographed riding a jackass in Khartoum at a time when Taunton boasted a Jackass Tavern, after the donkeys tethered outside that regularly brought brooms to the town from Broomfield.

Sammy remained a very popular and well-known figure in and around

Taunton even after his cricket-playing days were distant memory. Tales of his making the occupants of the amateurs 'perch' roar with laughter as he rattled off sporting and country-house stories in his loud, monopolistic voice were notorious. He also tended to monopolise the crease. I cite for example the 240 put on by Sammy and Vernon Hill at Taunton in 1898 that stood for 112 years as Somerset's highest fourth wicket partnership until broken by James Hildreth and Arul Suppiah 'set to', amassing 253 in the Kentish spa of Tunbridge Wells.

When Sammy died and was laid to rest close to the path in the old cemetery on Taunton's Wellington Road the town went into a state of mourning. The following beautiful tribute to Sammy, appeared in the press at the time of his death in 1931, inscribed "Joseph":

"The remembrance of him in his prime is the vision of a magnificent man. He may not have been 'clever' or 'erudite,' but he combined the courage of the heroes of old Homer with physical strength and kindliness, and to these ws joined the simplicity of a child.

"Only those who fielded with him can realise what he caught, what he stopped, and the ground he covered. His bowling when at its best was superb. Never tired and never beaten, ever happy and care-free, to have played cricket with Sammy in his golden prime is to have lived happy days and to have learnt the real meaning of courage, strength, and cheerfulness. To know that he is no longer in suffering and distress is to see in a tear-dimmed picture Lord's, the glorious sun, and Sammy at the Pavilion gate, bat in hand, cheered to the echo by a happy welcoming Bank Holiday crow."

The journalist R C Robertson-Glasgow wrote of him: "If you wanted to know Taunton, you walked round it with Sam Woods on a summer morning before the match. Sam was Somerset's godfather."

Anyway, with the story of Sammy's bat and memories of Grandpapa Harold in my head as well as the shouts from outside I belted to the tall brass umbrella stand by the front door. It was empty save for the knackered umbrella. The two cricket bats were missing. This was not good especially as it was crab apple season again.

Full of trepidation I popped my head outside and glanced anxiously down the street at the scene of upset. Lazy-eyed Marion was hobble-running axe in hands in pursuit of Lawrence, who at ten was my eldest. With Felix giggling beside him both ran towards home sanctuary. More importantly from what I could see in the onrush of small people, the bats thankfully seemed none the worse for wear save for the ciderous pith of splatted windfalls.

Apply a damp dishcloth and Shack and Trough would be none the wiser, I thought before stepping out to offer my humble apologises to the axe lady. "I promise the bats will be confiscated. You honestly won't be troubled by them again." And this was true, for later that day they would be returned from whence they came – the County Ground at Taunton.

At my own bequest, perhaps foolishly, I had been entrusted with the bats' safekeeping for a short while by Somerset Chief Executive Peter Anderson. One belonged to Andy 'Shack' Caddick, the other to a chap noted for his buffet appetite, Mark 'Trough' Lathwell and both were possessors of newish England caps. Their valued lumps of willow were to be props in an opening sequence for a documentary film cobbled together long before Andy had the latest of Somerset's County Ground triad of pavilions named in his honour, and disappeared up into the wide blue yonder after obtaining a helicopter pilot's licence; whereas Mark merely vanished into obscurity. And Heaven's knows why that was.

I was in the Bath crowd on a day Mark had repaid Somerset's faith in him following a season out with a knee injury and further one lacking any sort of form. Facing Yorkshire he excelled. Although not quite to the degree of a team-mate whose bat was another to earn its place in the cricket museum, and deserving of a glass case all to itself.

Mark began batting at 11.25 and had reached a breathtaking 98 at lunch when cruelly Jamie Cox made a presumably pre-arranged declaration with Somerset on 553 for five. In a way Mark had only himself to blame for not getting his hundred, perhaps by piercing the field with a replica of the sweet cuts he had been showing off throughout the morning, or even a slog, like the one moving him past 50 that landed on the roof of the Friends of Bath tent, reportedly causing a "ripple of Chardonnay". However, with five minutes to go before the interval he went down on one knee and launched into a six. The immaculate connection cleared the leg side marquees and hid under a car on the rugby ground. Heigh ho, a more modest effort, making a nuisance of itself in one of the tents, would have allowed another over.

Meanwhile at the other end Michael Burns, firing on all cylinders with his now preserved 'Gunn & Moore', hit the highest Somerset knock against that opposition. With slashing cuts of his own, and helped by generous bowling and Wiveyesque fielding, Michael reached 221 before limply sweeping a looping, gentle catch.

I suppose in truth this sort thing was what my film was about – Somerset's history told through gentle anecdotes. What came to light in its making was the warmth and affection exuded by former players. And as this was Somerset, it was noticeable that generous dollops of eccentricity overflowed.

The last time I saw Andy Caddick play was the first time Somerset took the field from the 'Caddy shack' in a Championship match. So of course it was appropriate that Andy himself played. Having spring pastured in Clevedon and Wiltshire, he was back in the side for his first game of the season and Yorkshire were batting. It was to be a poignant first morning's play. The Tykes were without Michael Vaughan, the Captain of England's lion-hearted Ashes winners in 2005, who minutes earlier had announced his cricketing retirement.

Among the straw hats, walking sticks and broadsheet crossword mutterings, the first trays of pints slopped in under hands of eleven o'clock drinkers. The crowd was building, building. Well, sort of. Two workmen in hard hats leaning on the top balcony rail of the ground's new flats, showed no signs of building anything content, as they were, to stump stare.

"This broadcast is brought to you by the Royal National Institute for the Blind," said the dulcet tone of Richard Walsh, blue short-sleeved shirt and striped Somerset tie to a growing band of listeners both at the ground and listening through internet stream.

Inside our hut it was the sweat that streamed despite the best efforts of a whirring desktop fan. We were sitting at the foot of the Ian Botham stand looking out across the twin churches, from a cramped timber-slatted 'potting-shed' whose 'Monkton Elm Plant and Pet Centre' sign-work emblazoning the front made me feel like an exhibit behind glass.

Semi-retired and armed with binoculars and a pocket crib book of cricketing facts Richard was an indispensable "bit of a freelance." On top of a two-hour commentary slot he sorted out the match scorecards, organised the programmes, wrote "odds and sods" for the *Western Morning News,* and did commentaries for the club website's video highlights.

Yorkshire won the toss and batted. Richard spoke of a "disturbed" scoreboard and gardening. Then, wicket! Joe Sayer, bowled Alfonso Thomas 8, Yorkshire 24 – 1. The Caddick pavilion offered an extended walk of shame. Moments later Alfonso sent down 'chin music', a bouncer cracking a Yorkshireman on the bonce, bringing giggles from a smattering of crowd and a geriatric cry of "Off wiv 'is 'ead."

"Ooer," said Richard. "We'll get an unsporting reputation again."

As a bleeding ear received attention to the delighted cries of wheeling seagulls, Richard and I swopped notes on a blacker day in Somerset sportsmanship, turning our reference books back to 1919 and an inauspicious tie. Sussex had travelled to Taunton a player short and Harold Heygate, there as a spectator, was pressed into service. Though since his last first-class cricket fourteen years before he had sustained leg wounds during the war and suffered badly from arthritis.

Somerset and Sussex scores were level when the ninth Sussex wicket fell. At that point, there was a hiatus. Historical account then has Heygate with pads strapped on top of his blue serge suit making a valiant, but fruitless attempt to reach the wicket from the Old Pavilion. After some minutes had elapsed without Heygate appearing to bat, someone on the Somerset side appealed and the umpire, a respected Test match official, ruled that Heygate was out, timed out. The stumps were pulled up and the match was a tie. Heygate was recorded as "out, absent". The decision caused controversy in the press and elsewhere, much of it focusing on the lack of civility to a wounded ex-serviceman.

On the spur of the moment I recalled another near timed-out incident. Rob Scanlon, who these days commentates for BBC Somerset and plays his cricket at Weston-super-Mare's Devonshire Park, had once been captain of Somerset U-17s for a couple of games. Playing at Rose Bowl in the same side as James Hildreth Rob had gone to the loo just before his team suffered an minor unexpected collapse. Once discovered and urgently told "Hurry up! You're in!" he sprinted down the pavilion steps with only one pad on, having grabbed a helmet and a bat. The Umpire, scrutinising at his watch, muttered. "Umm … you just made it." For his part, Rob obviously felt relieved.

From the shed I witnessed more contemporary struggling. Yorkshire belligerence had seemed to wear out Caddy in the field deep. When the chimes of Mary Magdalene church welcomed his first over after long absence, Yorkshire supporters greeted the ball thumping into the boundary boards. It was an early exchange that over four days saw over 1600 runs scored and culminated in a day of brilliance. By its end Yorkshiremen suggested leaving their team coach in a Taunton pub while they returned to plant potatoes in the pitch at Headingley.

Under ever-darkening skies the star turn was Weston-super-Mare's heavily tattooed Peter Trego who played the innings of his life that climaxed to one of those sporting days when those present are proud to say "I was there." He was one who knew his bat was of prime quality.

Peter's 54-ball century of biff-boff-bash enabled Somerset to pull off one of the most amazing County Championship wins in their history by a margin of four-wickets. It was the second highest successful run chase in the 145-year history of the County Championship with the home side reaching a massive target of 476 with 4.3 overs to spare.

You have to go back to 1925, when Middlesex made 502-6 to beat Nottinghamshire at Trent Bridge to find a bigger winning total by the side batting last in a Championship fixture.

So no one who was at the County Ground is likely to forget the game or Peter's incredibly clean hitting that brought him 9 sixes and 6 fours in 103 not out, coming in at number seven. Within moments of the players leaving the field there came a cloudburst that turned the County Ground into something resembling a boating lake. Those listening to the broadcast from the 'potting shed' heard a jingle declaring that Blackacre Farm free range eggs were "blooming lovely", accompanied by a staccato of roof drumming rain.

Justin Langer called the victory "a bit of a miracle", while Peter attributed his dramatic innings to "a few verbals" from Yorkshire seamer Ajmal Shahzad. He told the club website: "When I first went in, it was uppermost in my mind to just stay there, because I haven't been in the best of form in red ball cricket. Then Shahzad started winding me up and suddenly the ball turned from a pea into a balloon. I decided to let him have some!"

And so he did, swinging from the hip to record the fastest first class century of the season. With the considerable help of 'Marco Tresco' and Arul Suppiah, Somerset's effort was the fourth highest run-chase in first class cricket in England and the eighth highest in the world.

*

Yet memories fade from not just myself. They need recording. Now, with news in Somerset remaining positive my publisher's idea for me to keypad tap into such a rich vein of success wasn't to all intents and purposes a bad one. But he did have a caveat as he cuddled his chequebook in a state of prayer while saying, "Just keep it simple and lucid, don't muddy the waters, remember the grass roots, and don't go upsetting people into taking litigation."

Yet, his were helpful hints and probably worth heeding, especially when the thorny topic of bats raised itself once more at a family get together with my wife's German relatives.

Safe to say it was rather a civilised affair, a long way from Somerset's River Tone – a private barbecue luncheon on a patio the distance of a casual Trescothick banger over square leg from the Rhine. From a reedy speaker drifted Strauss's operetta *Die Fledermaus*. In a flight of whimsy it occurred to me that the music was the composition of Johann II. Back in Blighty we had a contemporary Strauss who was number one. Around the table beneath a large sun umbrella a small gathering ate sausages and kebabs in contemplative silence – a silence that I irreverently felt the desire to butt in on.

"In England our Herr Strauss is captain of our national cricket team. Although a Middlesex chap, the sound of balls flying from his bat thumping into boundary boards is music to our ears. When it comes to opening an England innings, he's our number one."

"Did you know we play cricket in Germany, too?" said Romulus, picking a homegrown tomato the colour of a new championship cricket ball.

"I know the Germans used to," I answered, going on to say that there had been a reasonable German cricket team in the 1930s. Indeed a minister of the Third Reich was even invited to Lord's to watch a test match. During his visit to England the minister tried to recruit some good county players, including one or two from Somerset, to go and play for club sides in and around Berlin. Volunteers, however, were short in coming forward, and thereafter the Germans diverted themselves with occupations other than those of the crease.

Romulus shrugged remorsefully. "Now our Deutcher team are not so good. Yet we are learning. We have just beaten Gibraltar and soon we hope to play Guernsey."

"Yes, but I hear we lost to Israel,'" chirped up Steffi, a nuclear physicist, "by 57 runnings." I was in reasonably well-informed company. "Must have been a match with a fair amount of needle," I offered jovially, only to receive what I considered an unfair glare from Steffi. Yet the match must have been up there with Wiveliscombe versus Brompton Ralph or, indeed, Somerset versus Gloucestershire. Surely not.

"Charles, will the book you say you are writing teach me about this game of cricket?" asked mother of two, Louisa, just flown in from Vienna.

My head filled with thoughts of cow corners, of chasing leather through buttercups and celandine and mingling with crowds filing through the gates of Sir Vivian or those of 'Big Bird' Garner. "Um, maybe," I answered, hesitantly.

"I mean will you say what you call the big stick the men use to hit the ball?" encouraged Louisa.

"What, the bat?"

"Ah, now I understand. We in Austria have great likings in common with you English."

"What likings?"

"'The bat', which we all call 'Die Fledermaus', and Strauss. Will you be writing about German cricket?"

"'fraid not. Just about cricket in Somerset."

"Somerset?"

It was time for another sausage and to lose myself to nostalgia, to keypad tap memories of crab apples tonked by the bats of Sammy, 'Shack' and 'Trough' thereby returning to basics, and, with respect to Grandpapa Harold's arcane recollections of poetry, the Taunton meads.

A Somerset Tribute from William Roe

"I doubt if any county ever had a happier band of cricketers than those who played for Somerset in the late eighties and nineties. There was never the slightest jealousy or ill-feeling, and though we often got beaten we also brought off many surprising victories. They were happy days, indeed, those twenty-one years during which I played for Somerset. What would I not give to have them all over again!"

Alphabet on the Somerset XI, 1892

A for the "averages" hard to beat,
B for the Batsmen so fleet on their feet,
C for the "centuries," Yorkshire's fate sealed,
Also for *Challen*, so deft in the field,
D for the "duck's-egg," that's never allowed,
E for the eagerness shown by the crowd,
F stands for *Fowler*, a good useful hitter,
G is for Gloucester, whose feelings are bitter,
H is for *Hewett* and *Hedley* and *Hill*,
I for the "innings" prolonged by their skill.
K for the "knocks," that poor *Newton* bore,
L for the Leg that is sometimes "before!"
M for the "maidens," our *Sammy's* just pride,
N is for *Nichols*, who ne'er bowls a "wide."
O for the "overs," that *Woods* makes renown'd,
P is for *Palairet*, a "clinker," all round!
Q for the quartet of bowlers so deadly,
S.M.J., *Nichols*, and *Hedley.*
R is for Robinson, ne'er caught at wicket,
S is for Somerset, *the* County of Cricket.
T is for *Tyler*, whose "slows," batsmen flurry,
The terror of Notts. and the envy of Surrey.
U for the Umpire, whose ankle's quite sore,
With stopping the drive that *Hill* meant for 4.
V for the "Varsity Blues" in the team
Of Cricketers verily they are the cream.
W the Wicket-keep, so smart with his catches,
X for the 'xtras, so rare in our matches.
Y for the Yorker, each bowler's ambition,
Z for the zeal which sent Notts. to perdition.

SIX

Doctors, Blisters and Butchery

"Few things are more deeply rooted in the collective imagination
of the English than the village cricket match."
Geoffrey Moorhouse (English journalist and author, 1931 –2009).

Back in 1946 the red and black colours of the Taunton & District Butcher's Association effectively sliced their way through the batting of the Bristol Meat Traders at the County Ground in the final of the now defunct SC Day Cup. Butchery of the ball was left to others.

So let it be said clubs come in all states of health, some rude, many not. Some have a smart, facility rich clubhouse, others a wooden shed. Some clubs have no home at all. Some are blessed with sightscreens. Others, the majority, have the ball leaving the bowlers arm only made visible by a backdrop of white, rain-washed, hillside sheep, the occasional statuesque egret, as on Dunster's river-end boundary, or whitewashed walls of urban brick. Some clubs, the rare ones, can boast the famous turning out for them.

And on this point I can relate an emotional moment within a 'Smokey' atmosphere on a July day in 2003. The County Ground was really quite full with folk having come to watch a Kent pub side bat against Somerset, and there was a tear my eye as I stood to applaud the incoming number 7 of Lashing Cricket Club.

Lawrence my eldest, raised on heroic stories and sensing the occasion, stood to clap too. On this, only his second visit in nine years to the County Ground, he was grinning from ear to ear. His first had been for a very mundane match against county opposition I can't even recall. "Oh God, we're losing," Vic Marks had uttered taking in the dressing and balcony body language as Lawrence and I tagged after him, me lugging a big camera and intent on doing player interviews, Lawrence intent on getting some autographs on his midget signature bat. "Not a good time," said Vic.

I looked around. In a a grump and sitting bare-torsoed on a dressing room bench beneath pegs hung heavy with dishevelled clothing and surrounded by desultory kit bags, Simon Ecclestone, left-handed bat who oddly bowled right-arm medium, glared first at my camera then at me from beneath a towel then buried his head. Clearly there were no *GQ* magazine front cover aspirations for him.

Nearby, an important cog of the rebuilding process at Taunton was nobbled and obviously missed that dismal day. Bum resting on a sink, his wan face grim despite his a richly deserved benefit season, injury-bedevilled sharp pacer 'Ghostie' Neil Mallender, appeared as ghostly in a white track-suit as he normally did in cricket whites. Jotting notes into a small black book, mouthing words that that were easy to lip-read but out of politeness impossible to record.

A TV in the corner played to itself.

And from what I could see, out on the balcony Somerset's new wicketkeeper, Helston-born Piran Holloway sat slumped in a chair, his feet resting on the rail. From the crowd there was silence apart from a broad Somerset heckle aimed at whichever unfortunate home batter had found himself in firing line. "It's a ball not a brick, it won't hurt yer bat! Hit the bloody thing!" Piran must have wished himself back in Cornwall, especially so when the secondary school party suddenly arrived in those depressed confines.

A host of fervent young lads were led en masse into the dressing room, each with a pen and an autograph book, clearly intent on the same mission as Lawrence. Ghostie hid in the loos. Simon emitted an audible obsenity from under his towel. Thankfully a padded up Andy Caddick came to the rescue by taking centre stage amongst the kit bags and benches, grudgingly doing the dutiful thing signing hither and thither, including, much to Lawrence's delight, the little hobbit willow.

Now, on his second visit, Lawrence had discovered an altogether different mood. So, I imagine, had Simon Ecclestone. He was by then playing for Saffron Walden. Ghostie had become an respected umpire. Such are the journeys of time.

My son and I weren't alone as we applauded that number 7. Everyone that I could see in the Taunton's old river end stand and elsewhere across the ground were behaving likewise as a fifty-one year old, wasp-waisted, muscular upper-bodied knight, neatly kitted out in the jet black garb, his cap set at a jaunty angle, swaggered to the crease twirling his bat. Just three overs of the allotted forty-five remained to be bowled.

Sir Vivian Richards, for yes it was he, proceeded to cruise to 16 off nine balls, hitting two fours and a languid on-driven six when, to the dismay of all concerned, the prematurely grey Andy Hurry, with the graceful leap of an Exe salmon, caught him in the deep. How annoying was that? The bloke wasn't even a pro. He was Somerset's ruddy ex-marine fitness instructor, for God's sake and heaven knows what made him tick. He had only ever graced Taunton Deane Cricket Club's Convent Field at the arse end of Vivary Park beyond the pitch and putt.

To cap it all, he had introduced yoga to the county's training regime to help with relaxation and flexibility, by all accounts. This was blooming Somerset, mate! The championship wooden spoon was being fought between us, Hampshire's hogs and the dismal Derbys. The mind could only boggle at the thoughts of Ian Blackwell, KwaZulu-Natal's Gary Gilder, Nixon McLean or the apparently uber-fit Mike Burns doing sun salutations at dawn. How was I to know that by that season's close Andy's humble club team were to be crowned Somerset Premier Division Champions, or that he had encouraged Marcus Trescothick to training on the previous Christmas Eve?

Anyway, in the midst of my mental rant, so departed the man that a county professional once described as "the kind of batting genius I pray I compete against never again in my suddenly very inadequate career".

However, I took comfort in my lad having seen the legend who that morning had officially opened the new 'Sir Viv Richards Gates' at the ground's Priory Bridge entrance. The iron was a fitting tribute to nine Somerset centuries in 1985 including a five hour 322 against Warwickshire described as "unabated butchery" uninfluenced by the tripe, giblets and chops profession of Peter Denning's Dad, and had followed on from seven tons in 1977 and 1981. Smokey, with his smoting and stroking, had just appeared to get better and better until his abrupt and bitter departure in 1986 that followed the Shepton Mallet kerfuffle.

Yet, neither the politic of future reconciliation nor a gate opening ceremony could have been in Sir Viv's wildest imaginings when, arriving as a young Antiguan without a work permit at Heathrow in 1974, he alarmingly confronted immigration officials. Fortunately, Len Creed, erstwhile farmer,

Bath bookmaker and Somerset committee member, had helpfully intervened. Len was duty bound to protect his golden asset, 'discovered' while on holiday in Antigua the year before. The chance encounter led to Somerset signing the man who was to become known as Smokey and for Len a deluge of free cider pints. But first things first. The star of Antiguan and Leeward Islands cricket was on his way towards Bath to add his name to Lansdown Cricket Club's first team. The club, once called "the MCC of the West" and older even than Beckington Cricket Club out Frome way, was the launching pad for Viv to find his feet playing in English conditions. He was there for a year while he qualified for Somerset.

Later, during the 1980s, after he had played his benefit match in a Somerset side playing against Bristol City footballers on a drop in wicket at Ashton Gate, Sir Viv was interviewed by the Trinidadian-born newsreader and journalist Sir Trevor McDonald. Sir Viv recalled some nightly discomforts:

"When I first came to the West Country I was put up with a guy from Barbados. This guy was the kind of West Indian who must have created the impression that he had a large house. All he had was one little room and the bit I was supposed to sleep in was where he kept his steel drums. I like steel drums a lot, but I didn't want to sleep with them. To make matters worse, they would go out to parties and come back late at night, make a lot of noise and try and squeeze the steel drums into the tiny room where I was sleeping.

"For a long time that was Bath for me." Much later the rumour spread that for away games Viv had a girl near every county ground to stay with, so making a saving on hotel bills.

In order to afford to play for Lansdown, a club with a very big facility-rich clubhouse, chaps had to earn their keep. Some would have given a penny for the thoughts of Smokey, assistant groundsman, as he pushed the pitch roller, blisters on his hands, or cut Lansdown's grass, knowing what nightfall offered.

Was he aware that he was part of a long tradition of notable groundsmen? Landsdown's first had been a gamekeeper called John Sparks, or so says Landown's chronicler, Dr Bradfield. What is undisputed is that John was Somerset's first professional cricketer. Described in Arthur Haygarth's *Scores and Biographies* as "a hard, slashing, hitter" and "a splendid bias bowler of no great pace" John was hired in 1830. Giving up rearing pheasants for the shooting season to scythe the outfield, his additional remit was to bowl dibbly-dobblies to the members, gents who were more than willing to meet John's wages just so long as he did all the manual stuff. According to his daughter, John's mates weren't very impressed by his cricketing appetite. He played against their wishes. She was reticent to say any more, perhaps herself believing that he would have been better off with his game birds and potting rabbits and crows.

The only game Viv knew, on the other hand, was cricket. And whatever may have crossed his mind, he was nurturing hallowed ground once the haunt of the intimidating, the la-di-da and an awesome set of very bright brothers, the Graces – the coroner Edward Mills known by his initials as EM, and the two doctors, the famous William Gilbert or WG, and Henry.

With WG being only fourteen years old at the time, he and his brothers took all the wickets between them and probably never gave any inkling of coming off. Such energy was something WG never seemed to be without and was obviously an asset as he developed into the famous aggressive batsman. Pity that he chose to play for Gloucestershire. However, he wasn't without generosity towards folk with a Somerset leaning. When Gloucestershire once bowled Somerset out for 57 in under an hour he gave the match ball, with a wry smile it's said, to a Somerset supporter.

"I don't like blocking; you only get three," he once asserted. And true to form, the Prebendary Archdale Wickham, Somerset's gauntleted stumper, counted only four balls that passed the doctor's bat during WG's hundredth hundred at Bristol in 1895, an event celebrated by champagne so revitalising that he proceeded on to make 288 in three hundred and twenty minutes.

AA Thompson was moved to write: "What do I think of WG? Why, I have never seen his like and never shall. I tell you my opinion, which is that WG should never be put underground. When he dies his body ought to be embalmed and permanently exhibited in the British Museum as 'The colossal cricketer of all time'." Lansdown could be rightly proud of providing the nursery for the man Sammy Woods called "an artful old toad".

And spare a thought for the Prebendary. Not only did he have to put up with WG's rear view that year but worse, he also had to suffer the bum belonging to Archie MacLaren whose 424 for Lancashire at Taunton remains the only quadruple hundred made by a player actually born in Blighty. "Taunton is killing cricket," Archie went on record as saying. One must add though that Worcestershire's Graeme Hick considered himself to be an Englishman when he managed 405 not out at Taunton in May 1988. He hit 11 sixes and 35 fours, a carnage I was lucky enough to witness and wince at.

But as records go, originally formed as far back as 1825, Lansdown is readily acknowledged as being the oldest and first organised club in the county. Indeed, many have argued, Somerset County Cricket Club came indirectly from Lansdown. And certainly when Somerset was officially formed in 1875 it was led by the captain of Landsdown

Yes, it's appreciated that ten years earlier, the first attempt at a county side was made with the formation of Yeovil and County Cricket Club. But did it deserve the accolade of giving rise to Somerset? Categorically no. Despite Yeovil & County playing a 'county' fixture against the Gentlemen of Devon the match was abandoned due to rain. Before that they performed poorly in their opening matches against local club sides, and on one occasion, even lost three players to their opposition the day before the match was scheduled to begin.

As a piece of useless information, an oil painting called 'Gloucester v Somerset 1831' depicts underarm bowling seemingly amusing a smattering of genteel spectators in top and hats and tails. However, cricket's history boffins are adamant that the cricket match is really between Cliftonians and Lansdown, and they cite the setting as being the Duke of Beaufort's country pile.

Indeed, with a limited number of other organised clubs to play, fixtures were few and far apart in the founding years, with matches being played against Clifton, Sidmouth and Teignmouth. The Bath club even played a United England eleven in 1860, a team created by John Wisden, a small chap bowling quickish snickworthy off-cutters lauded as the best all-rounder in the country, and who four years later became famed for launching the eponymous *Wisden Cricketers' Almanack.*

With United England, Lansdown faced opposition from not only JW but also Thomas Hayward, said to be the finest professional batter in the country, and bizarrely, Julius Caesar – a name not feared in Bath since 55 BC when the "Pennyquick fault' had been noticed as making for hot spa waters rather than either a defect in local batting technique or a rupture caused by the exertions of catching.

In that year of the second Caesar's coming came also the first recorded occasion of a Gentlemen of Somerset side playing. They travelled down to Culm Vale to take on the Gentlemen of Devon, and earned a draw.

More recently Landsdown and Viv have met with mixed fortunes.

In 2010 Lansdown won the Butcombe sponsored North Somerset Cricket Conferences Twenty-20 Cup in a dramatic last over finish by 3 wickets over Whitchurch. It was a case of Sparkesian swipes into calf rather than cow corner for a young lad called Dan Veal. With an unbeaten 29 he was the Combe Park club hero as wickets tumbled around him. Set under five an over to win, Lansdown had appeared to be coasting to victory, before Whitchurch bowler Rob Bailey caused carnage. So for Lansdown it was happy days. Viv, however, must have had lingering thoughts on a dark night far removed from his Landsdown groundings.

In the 'Bearin'Up' Stodger, a regular bibbler and looking tickled pink, chuckled into his cider. He had discovered some old foreign gossip dating back to end of the 1990s. Viv, whose liking for the ladies was on a par with that Sammy Woods and of Stodger himself, had had a fling with Neena Gupta, an Indian stage and film actress of no celebrity standing in either field. The Mumbai field she had strolled onto full of flirtatious intent was of a cricket nature. The West Indies were there taking part in the 1987 Cricket World Cup.

India's media elite stood aghast as nine months later Ms Gupta gave birth to a baby girl "boldly and unrepentantly – without marriage and without even announcing the name of the child's father". Suddenly Nena found herself catapulted to sub-continent fame, and not just because of her roles becoming raunchy, sexy and teasingly bold.

The finger of suspicion pointed towards Viv and the international media, too, took a keen and amused interest in his escapade. Even then, Neena remained in the backwaters of the media world. It was only when an intrepid journalistic hound, Pritish Nandy, obtained a xerox of her child's birth certificate that clearly mentioned the name of Viv as the father of a baby girl, Masaba, that Neena became an overnight celebrity. More so, when the birth certificate was published in the *Illustrated Weekly of India*.

History will just have it, in Somerset anyway, that Viv far removed from the Graces was gated. In Stodger's opinion, and in that of Somerset supporters everywhere, Indian affairs were best left to the spin of Murali Kartik, who in turn may prefer to leave thoughts of yoga to Andy Hurry, now the county's much vaunted first team coach.

An Historic Thank You To Sir Viv

THE GILLETTE CUP FINAL 1979

NORTHAMPTONSHIRE v SOMERSET
At Lord's Ground, Saturday 8 September, 1979
Umpires: DJ Constant and JG Langridge
Northamtonshire won the toss and elected to field.

Somerset innings

*BC Rose		b Watts	41
PW Denning	c Sharp	b Sarfraz	19
IVA Richards		b Griffiths	117
PM Roebuck		b Willey	14
IT Botham		b T. Lamb	27
VJ Marks		b Griffith	9
GI Burgess	c Sharp	b Watts	1
D Breakwell		b T. Lamb	6
J Garner		not out	24
+DJS Taylor		not out	1
Extras (Byes 5, leg-byes 3, no balls 3)			11
Total for 8			269

Did not bat: KF Jennings.

Fall of wickets: 1-34, 2-95, 3-145, 4-186, 5-213, 6-214, 7-219, 8-268.

Northamptonshire bowling: Sarfraz: 12-3-51-1, Griffiths: 12-1-58-2, Watts: 12-1-34-2, T. Lamb:12-0-70-2, Willey: 12-2-45-1.

Northamptonshire innings

G Cook		run out	44
W Larkins	lbw	b Garner	0
RG Williams	hit wicket	b Garner	8
AJ Lamb	st Taylor	b Richards	78
P Willey	c Taylor	b Garner	5
TJ Yardley	c Richards	b Burgess	20
*G Sharp		b Garner	22
Sarfraz Narwaz		not out	16
TM Lamb		b Garner	4
BJ Griffiths		b Garner	0
PJ Watts		Absent Hurt	
Extras (Byes 6, leg-byes 9, wides 5, no balls 7)			27
Total for 9			224

Fall of wickets: 1-3, 2-13, 3-126, 4-138, 5-170, 6-186, 7-218, 8-224, 9-224.

Somerset bowling: Garner: 10.3-3-29-6, Botham: 10-3-27-0, Jennings: 12-1-29-0, Burgess: 9-1-37-0, Marks: 4-0-22-0, Richards: 9-0-44-1, Breakwell: 2-0-9-0.

Somerset won by 45 runs.

Some notes about this historic match:

This match completed Somerset's first major success in county cricket since becoming First-class in 1891.

It was Somerset's 41st match in the Gillette Cup, and their third against Northamptonshire. The two previous matches were at Northampton in 1967 and 1970, Somerset winning both.

Somerset had previously reached the final in 1967 and 1978, having reached the semi-finals in 1966, 1970, 1974 and 1977.

Sir Vivian Richards scored only the third century ib the final. The others were 146 by Geoffrey Boycott for Yorkshire in 1965 and 126 by Clive Lloyd for Lancashire in 1972.

Richards reached 50 in 80 minutes and 100 in 167 minutes with nine fours. He eventually hit eleven fours, having come in during the 7th over and was out in the 60th. When he had 17 in the 17th over he dived a long way to avoid a run out. For several minutes he appeared to have severely damaged his back. However, he recovered to play a match winning innings.

He found four useful partners, With Rose he added 61 in 18 overs; Roebuck helped to add 50 in 13 overs; Botham's lively 27 made the stand 41 in 7 overs; and after three wickets had fallen in three successive overs, Garner shared a vital partnership of 49 in 8 overs.

Garner took a wicket in each of his first two overs but then AJ Lamb, adding 113 in 32 overs with Cook changed the course of the match. During this time, Jennings, with a fine spell of 12 overs for only 29 runs held them importantly in check. The critical partnership Was broken when Cook, trying a second run to long-on, was beaten by Roebuck's throw.

Perhaps the final turning point came when Lamb was dismissed for 78 in 33 overs with nine fours. A fast off-side stumping by Taylor off Richards made the score 170 for 5 in 46 overs with 100 needed in 14 overs.

As Watts had had his hand badly damaged by a Richards drive just before he was out he was unable to bat.

Garner came back and the last 21 deliveries took four wickets for 9 runs making his final figures 6-29, the best ever achieved in a Gillette Cup final. However, Sir Vivian Richards was named Man of the Match by adjudicator C Washbrook.

As winners Somerset won £5,500. As Runners-Up Northamptonshire won £2,500.

The thousands of Somerset supporters who had travelled to Lord's left Somerset in dull weather, and halfway to London a heavy mist and low cloud produced some gloom. In the event it was a perfect, warm summer's day.

Middling Wobbles

Rabbits and Buttercups

"When the rabbit has escaped, comes advice."
Proverb.

"Why are tailenders called rabbits?" asked Phil Tufnell on Test Match Special, so starting a jovial debate with Christopher Martin-Jenkins and Vic Marks to keep chins up around a clatter of English wickets at the Kensington Oval. There was agreement that it was much to do with non-proficient batsmen being likened to timorous creatures caught wide-eyed in headlights. Rabbits suited this analogy admirably, much better than rats, an offered alternative name for tailenders. Although coupled with "sinking ships", rats struck a cord. Before I fell into a self-absorbed reflection at my own ineptitude with the willow CMJ put the cat among the Oval pigeons, mentioning that in his own experience it was extremely hard to eradicate rabbits.

We in Somerset could proudly support that view. Led by Marcus Trescothick, the latest of the line that began with Reverend Stirling Cooksley Voules from Middle Chinnock, the county's cricketers had tasted a recent sweet run of success begun out of sheer cussedness after a Durham wag named Somerset "batting bunnies".

In reality rabbits were an accepted part of Somerset life. During the First World War the County Ground became overrun with the hoppity creatures. Many an observer considered that the old scoreboard couldn't cope with the numbers. Such copulating and birthing was truly disconcerting to polite society. Burrowing though was a practical problem of an acute nature that needed someone of Sammy Woods stature to solve. He did so by knocking one day on groundsman Ernie Robson's Taunton door. "It's these bloody rabbits, Robbie. You're a good shot. Get rid of 'em m'dear."

Without more ado Ernie, a melancholic Yorkshireman with a severe moustache, set off, 12 bore under his arm, and faithful spaniel at his heel. The dog did the flushing out and Ernie did the popping – a massacre of dozens.

In the *Three Ferrets,* as the Brompton Ralph portacabin clubhouse is lovingly known, high on the plateau of one of Exmoor's foothills called Pitsford Hill, I hoped Roy Takle the club's heart and soul was listening to the Tuffers' instigated discussion.

In my mind's eye, the clubhouse weathervane moved imperceptibly in the sultry breeze. It's a fine piece of ironmongery showing a metal black-capped batsman down on one knee upon his wind direction arrow hitting the red ball that tops the vane's pivot. Inside the clubhouse I imagined Roy pinching deserved respite from the sweated ardours of ground duty lounging in a white T-shirt and scruffy grey chinos, his Nike soled feet resting on a stool. Since 1966 the club had been his life. Reportedly he had been a damn fine player who had revelled in being captain for twenty-five years and doubled up as fixtures secretary, club secretary, and coach. Probably more importantly, Roy was also acclaimed as probably the finest living groundsman in Somerset.

And as groundsmen in these parts went, Roy was still a whippersnapper. Thin, wiry, Ken Baker, who passed on in 2003, had looked after the Winsford pitch and boiled the Saturday tea kettle for years until he finally retired aged ninety. It was readily agreed that that pitch by the vicarage, railed in to keep off the cows, was a real beauty. Not for Ken a wicket that might pong of 'eau de vache' like one of Cecil Buttle's, the Somerset groundsman at around the time of the Coronation festivities.

In 1953 a Buttle wicket was as ruddy as the face of an Exmoor farmer and as barren of grass as Berrow Beach. This was nowt to do with sandstone soil and much more to do with a topping of bull's blood and cow manure spread across the pitch with a watering can. Cecil had the brainwave of camouflaging his bovine concoction by spreading grass cuttings and rolling them in. The smelly wicket followed on after Somerset were beaten by Lancashire with nearly an hour left on the first day, every ball bowled appearing to remove a clod of earth as it pitched. On reflection the mixture's painstaking application was a far more sensible solution to Air Vice-Marshall Taylor query as to what the groundsman meant to do. Initially, Cecil's mortified reply was "Hang myself, sir".

As for Ken, a good roller and a mower sufficed for his groundsman's duties. Neither was he a cricketer. The only leather he ever chased after were hunt saddles as he tried to keep up while following the Devon & Somerset Staghounds. This probably accounted for why his Morris Traveller that was more than a third of Ken's age at the time of his death only had 77,000 miles on the clock.

However, on Roy pitches a mere soft handed forward defensive push could be guided for four over an outfield as smooth as glass, something that I delighted in after eagerly agreeing to make up last minute numbers for a rare outing with Lydeard St Lawrence seconds. Sadly, my carefully accumulated 7 runs were not enough to avoid a collective defeat by a goodly hundred odd.

Anyway, had Roy caught Tuffers cuniculus question his thoughts would most likely have turned to early morning lamp lit rabbit shooting accompanied by his mate Maurice who brought along his Jack Russell. Around 4 am the trio would visit the clubhouse where the men would down a glass or two. Often Roy would fall asleep on a bench and have to go dishevelled straight from the pavilion to work. Not in any way, however, am I insinuating that as a groundsman Roy was a guddler of Godsmarkian proportions.

A drunkard, Godsmark was the county's first official groundsman, drawn from the era when the County Ground hosted the Somerset Lawn Tennis Championship, cycling championships, an archery competition, and even a performance of Pygmalion. Engaged for a year Godsmark didn't take his duties very seriously although he did pester successfully for a shower to be built to wash his horse, the puller of the mowers and which wore leather pads on its hooves so as not to dent the pitch too much. The 25 shillings Godsmark earned a week he spent on booze.

Safe to say, Roy only bibbled and his unstinting club work was voluntary. It was Maurice who tongue-in-cheek named the prefab *The Three Ferrets*, after the pub in the 1980s' TV advert for John Smith's bitter that featured a Jack Russell, Gordon Rollings, Charlie Pemberton and Jane Freeman with the claim that the beer was "nicer than bunny-wunnies".

Yet it was thanks to Roy that there was any semblance of a clubhouse or even a ground in the first place. And there lies the story. Born in 1942, the same year as the aptly christened county wicketkeeper Derek Somerset Taylor, Roy's early life had been in a council house in a row of five from which the entire Brompton Ralph team was sourced.

Back then all employment was local. Home games were played at a farm three quarters of mile from the present ground. Then, for reasons best known to himself, the farmer kicked the club out. But then again these things happen. Take Bathford Cricket Club for instance. They had to go elsewhere simply because of a trivial dispute with Mr Beazer, their farming landlord, over the size of the playing area.

So in relation to Brompton Ralph in 1966 as England thought about football, and years before the portacabin's arrival, the question was: What to do? In a manner Sammy Woods would have been proud, Roy found a solution. After a word in the ear of another farmer chap, Arthur Hews who tended Pitsford Hill, Roy's boys were offered sanctuary.

But there was still the problem of the pitch that was knee high with buttercups and celandines, the incentive for Roy's venture into groundsmanship. Aided by an ancient finger mower, he and his brother Kevin took turns in cutting a path so that the batmen could poddle to and from the wicket. Batsmen just put up with the fact that many a middled cricket ball didn't receive its full merit due the slowing properties of the remaining yellow flowering vegetation. Many a shot, instead of raising scatterings of applause, only raised pollen.

Not that Brompton Ralph had much batting strength. Wary of this, Roy always inserted the opposition whenever he had the chance "just to make a game of it". Humming or even singing Donovan's *Mellow Yellow* under their breath, home batters meandered between the flowers towards the crease to take guard.

When a sit-on Webb and then a new-fangled Aller replaced the finger mower matters improved. It only took two and a quarter hours to box up the clippings. However, there was still a Spartan lack of amenities. By necessity teams had to change at the edge of a pitch from their civvies into whites stained the colour of tumeric. It was most tiresome.

Finally, long before grand improvements became the design of the County Ground, a right and proper decision was made that a changing room would be a sensible Brompton acquisition, and Roy had the bright idea where he could cadge one.

Purposefully, and in the belief that bygones should be bygones, he returned to the club's evicting farmer to persuade him to recycle in a more down beat fashion to Henry VIII's recycling of Lindisfarne priory to make Holy Island castle. A twenty-foot by ten, defunct, deep litter chicken house would do Roy nicely after being spring cleaned of feather, fowl poo and straw. For an age it hadn't been up to scratch for West Somerset hens to cluck proud clucks over brown eggs in.

After a tow and a tug, and a face-lift of a new white painted hard board front to hide the off-putting chook hatches from the more discerning of local cricketers, the house was found to be really quite accommodating.

A small wooden shed followed in which to do the all important teas. A year later, most importantly, came a ladies toilet. Suddenly Brompton Ralph had all mod cons and team strength began to grow, as did the quality of the teas. This I understood was down to the sudden influx of sandwich, scone and cake makers, women without whom the club couldn't function.

When the West Somerset League was formed in 1976, Brompton Ralph were the first winners, and they have been champions nine times since. And as for the West Somerset League Knockout Cup, well, they won that six times as well, with the 'double' being achieved in 1986 and 1989. Celebratory stuff.

One sultry Wednesday evening not long ago I sat and chatted to Roy as he slumped contentedly. I didn't want to spoil the moment by hinting at a barren patch of success over the past decade. And I'm glad that I didn't. Safe from the summer evening midge clouds, Roy divulged his club's major stroke of good fortune.

In her will a philanthropic local lady known as Mrs Bragg left a man that she had never met one hundred West Somerset acres, an undisclosed sum of money and shares in Whitbread brewery. The beneficiary of this windfall of wonderfulness was Jim Hews, Captain of Lincolnshire and also of the Warwick and Coventry Cricket Club. Jim in turn wrote a cheque for £7,756 made payable to Brompton Ralph to purchase a port-a-cabin clubhouse to replace the infamous former chicken residence. Long gone, the shady spot where it had once stood was now occupied by a smart gang mower.

Roy broke off our tittle-tattle to look out through a clubhouse window in admiration as Brompton Ralph's opener Ben Criblin was giving it some pongo. Balls bulged the extensive, above hedge, protective boundary nets that do a fair imitation of the famous giant Chinese fishing nets of Kerala's city of Cochin. "I think Ben's chapel," said Roy scratching at his nose. "He won't play Sundays. Pity, we need him all the time really."

"Johnny Lawrence was like that," I responded after a moment's thought, "chapel." The balding, tiny specimen of a gentleman leg-spinner of Yorkshire roots had joined Somerset in the year after the Second World War ended and signed off in his last season with a hat-trick and a half century against his native Yorkshire, a match in which Somerset was skippered by Yorkshireman George Tordoff and Brian Close hit a match winning century for, I regret to say, Yorkshire.

When Johnny's benefit year finally came around he refused to organise the traditional Sunday games with village teams. Such frivolity, he claimed, offended against his "strict religious convictions". As a reward for putting his principles first a host of sympathisers sent him money. Indeed, there was so much dosh that his service to the county was amply recognised. As he left Somerset to play Lancashire League cricket having taken up a contract to be the professional at Haslingden Cricket Club two Australians came the other way, Colin McCool and Bill Alley.

Of course Johnny had many fans but surely there was none greater than a dour bespectacled Yorkshireman down in the West Country doing "some research". In his early sixties with receding chin and donned in a buttoned-up, dour maroon and grey 'best' cardigan, I came across him by chance amidst thick library tomes of statistics, a dicta-phone close to hand, sifting through similar looking snap shots of a face that I recognised.

"Johnny Lawrence, eh?" I said, attempting to be conversational.

Failing to get any response other than a grunt I foolishly persevered. "Fan of Johnny, were you?"

"I believe I remember watching him bowl at Headingly once. He was my hero," said the serious fellow blurting out the latter statement with such force that it was a tad scary. Here unquestionably was a worshipper, an idolising zealot. One that then told me he thought himself "a brilliant writer", and who voiced his serious intent of writing a biography of Johnny with a title something along the lines of 'Jovial Genius'.

"If you're looking for photos there's a grand one of Johnny blowing his nose under a sign saying 'reserved'," I offered light-heartedly. "In front of Neath's corrugated iron roofed pavilion as he comes out to field against Glamorgan. 1949, I think. Gimblett's having a giggle. It's on the cover of one those books compiled by the Somerset Cricket Museum."

"I didn't know," said the Worshipper, earnestly searching for a biro and a scrap of paper.

"Also did you know," I continued, putting my oar in even further, "Johnny was part of Somerset's worst batting debacle in their entire history. A second innings disaster against Gloucestershire."

"Why should that matter? Johnny was known for being a bowler not a batsman," snapped the Worshipper quicker than a mousetrap.

"Well Somerset had a ruddy long tail then, he came in at number 4." I said, giving as good as I got, recalling the history of a true bunny-hopper day. "And … and Johnny top scored in the first inning with 34, but failed to trouble the scorers in the second. In that match Somerset's batters emerged not so much from the pavilion as from a burrow." And indeed it was so. All in all, apart from wicky Frank Lee's 17, it was a very 'noughty' performance. Six of the best. Rollo Meyer was among them, the founder of Millfield School, in unsurprisingly his only year as captain. And Somerset's No. 11 was called Hazell, which really smacked of novel heroes drawn from *Watership Down*.

"Did you know he had two sons and three daughters?" said the Worshipper redressing the balance of useless knowledge. "And that his surviving son Steve runs the Johnny Lawrence Lordswood Cricket School? That's near Tadcaster. Steve's my cricket coach."

As much as I tried I just couldn't imagine the Worshipper playing cricket at all, let alone on a Sunday. "Are you chapel?" I asked, curious.

"What's that got to do with anything?" he said, now giving indications of becoming violent on having rammed a mini-tape the wrong way round into his dicta-phone.

"Oh, just that wherever Johnny may have batted down the order he had an 'Angell' above him."

The Worshipper's eyes narrowed, scrutinising me.

"Opener Frederick Leslie Angell from Norton St Phillip. Good luck with your project" I said, and beat a belated retreat.

Chapel or not, Ben reached his hundred within twelve overs by tonking a flagging Bagborough bowler for 6 somewhere deep into a hedge. A blackbird took flight chack-chacking its discontent and several fielders mooched hands in pockets. Others, after leaf-kicking and stick-prodding green density, declared "lost ball". For Ben, reward for his services that evening would likely be a clubhouse pint of orange and soda on Roy.

The clubhouse itself was smart, and no spiked shoes were allowed inside so was it nice to witness a young lad in a shirt declaring '28 Durston Somerset' on the back, crawl on hands a knees across the thin carpet to obtain a replacement ball from behind the bar. "Good evening, Mr Durston," I said.

The perspiring shirt wearer looked up at me with a beaming adolescent smile. "Wes gave the shirt away before he became a Unicorn."

"Good heavens," I said, feigning astonishment. "And to think Keith Parsons became such a fabled creature, too."

Roy's life had yet to reach fabled proportions, but these days he still basks in a success for which he should rightly be proud. "2005 was a good year," he mused, regaining my attention. "Got a hip replacement. Off for six weeks, I was. Mind you, also getting the 'Community Groundsman of the Year' award in a national competition made me feel a whole lot better. Had to go all the way up to Lord's to receive it. I was a bloomin' VIP." Then with a chuckle he went on to say that he and his wife Lillian were late for the official ceremony. Roy's BMW suffered a motorway blow out at Leigh Delamere and the offending tyre had to be eventually changed at Reading. All the while the Lord's dignitaries in the Michael Holding box could only twiddle their thumbs until eventually the former Indian wicketkeeper Farouk Engineer did the honours of handing Roy the trophy.

"Going up to Lord's must have felt like a pilgrimage," I said.

"Well, I live at Pilgrim Cottage, don't I?" replied Roy, giving another chuckle. And with that he 'upped and offed', saying as exiting through the door, "Stay where you are. There's something I want to show you. Won't be a minute."

I watched him hobble over to his home on the boundary edge, and waited. And waited. A West Somerset minute is more like twenty. On reappearing Roy held something that seemed to be very special. It was a small box like those used by jewellers to contain precious trinkets of great expense. And Roy's box did indeed contain an item to cherish. It was a gold medal, an 'Oscar', dated 2006.

"Brian Rose presented it to me at the County Ground," Roy said, gazing down like Gollum at the Queen's Golden Jubilee Award for services to cricket. He was as proud as proud could be. And probably just as proud as Millfield prodigy Craig Kieswetter was when he showed off his T20 World Cup Winners' medal to all and sundry at the County Ground.

A week or two earlier England had humbled Australia by seven wickets in the final at Kensington Oval, Bridgetown, Barbados. Although it's best not to dwell on Man of the Match Kieso's comical dismissal, castled stepping away from a straight one, victory came with almost anti-climactic ease after thirty-five barren years without a trophy. The downside of fickle celebrity meant my lad Felix was deleted overnight as one of Kieso's Facebook friends. Felix almost needed a consoling man-hug from me.

Roy had no such issues. Facebook didn't register in his consciousness. What mattered to Roy was that by becoming a rural celebrity the 'powers-that-be' took his plans for the future of Brompton Ralph seriously.

Tom Graveney, uncle of the former England chairman of selectors, David Graveney who crossed the county divide from Gloucestershire in 1991 to play a solitary season for Somerset, had already been and sorted out the laying of an artificial wicket. And a fine chap from the MCC planned to visit to make an general inspection and propose giving a grant to develop another pitch on the ground. Heady times, indeed. I left Roy planning a pig roast to help fill the coffers of his latest ambition, a new pavilion.

On a Saturday evening a week or so later the subject of Roy cropped up again. Wivey had beaten Brompton Ralph convincingly in a match not lacking sporting camaraderie. With Wivey's stalwart of the middle order storming, black cloud above his head, back to the clubhouse adjudged ell bee to a blinder of a decision, Lee, Brompton's imposing chubber of a twenty-something cider drinker enquired, "Sorry umpire, but how can you give a player out when you're not looking at the stumps?"

However, whatever distraction might have been caused by the circling of predatory buzzards, the iffy raised finger didn't affect the end result. Wivey's 169 for 9 played Brompton's 73 all out, and Dennis, Wivey's captain and opening bat, was cock-a-hoop, especially as he and Roy worked in the same Highways Department office.

On the eve of the match Dennis had overheard Roy boast that Wivey would get "a spankin". Come Monday morning Dennis made it his mischievous intention to mention something about a load of bunnies. What a rat, I thought.

A Nadir of Bunnydom

GLOUCESTERSHIRE v SOMERSET
Ashleigh Down Ground, Bristol, August 1947.

Gloucestershire 244 all out and 195 for 9 declared
Somerset 98 all out and 25 all out
Gloucestershire won by 316 runs.

Somerset second innings

MM Walford		b Lambert	5
M Coope		b Lambert	1
HE Watts	lbw	b Barnett	0
J Lawrence	c Neale	b Barnett	0
+FS Lee		b Goddard	17
MF Tremlett	c Emmett	b Goddard	1
*RJO Meyer	lbw	b Goddard	0
GR Langdale		b Goddard	0
AW Wellard	c Parker	b Goddard	0
HFT Buse		not out	1
HL Hazell	lbw	b Cook	0
Extras			0
Total (all out, 12.4 overs)			25

Fall of wickets:
1-5, 2-6, 3-6, 4-6, 5-24, 6-24, 7-24, 8-24, 9-24, 10-25 (12.4 overs)

EIGHT

Of Kit Bags, Odd Quacks and Fishing Nets

"He who would travel happily must travel light."
Antoine de Saint-Exupery (French writer and aviator, 1900 - 1944).

Sometimes, for the sake of self-respect, one needs to apportion blame. And I blamed the 'Hero' for my being on the periphery, boots scuffing grass inside the boundary rope, long leg stationed though my own legs were short. My heart was heavy, though perhaps more accurately, my tummy was. I arrived at grounds by myself, a mercenary paid by sausage rolls, sandwiches, and cream and jam topped scones. Wivey or Lydeard St Lawrence could happily have me, a willing addition to make up numbers, to trot considerably less nimbly than a forest creature after a ball, and to swish, swipe and nurdle with something considerably less than aplomb.

The 'Hero' in question was no guest player drawn from Somerset's Golden Age of one day success invited to ply his skills to the benefit of a rag-tail village team. Like of say Joel Garner, a man whose first wicket for Somerset was the Australian opener Richard McCosker, and the man who saved Somerset by the skin of their teeth beside the A303 from a first loss on a village green after coming to the rescue against Sparkford, and who, for a halcyon afternoon that's still talked about today, turned out for Wivey in a match at Bridgetown.

Perhaps that was as a favour to Bugsy for tending lovingly to the mechanical needs of his Jaguar motor car, or perhaps Bugsy hadn't been too specific which Bridgetown he had meant when he popped Joel the initial invitation. Due consideration would have made it clear Wivey club funds didn't lend themselves to much of a travel budget and that as a result Bridgetown, Exmoor was a very different place to Bridgetown, Barbados.

Anyway, however it came about, caught on the hop with his head in the clouds, Joel had said, "Yes, man."

And to his immense credit Joel did turn up at the pretty cricket ground beside the River Exe where there is a thatched pavilion so quintessentially English, so unique, that it gains mention in Jonathan Rice's *Book of Pavilions*. Indeed, in 2002 Bridgetown Cricket Club was voted the 'Loveliest Cricket Ground in England' by Wisden, and in 2008 won the *Daily Telegraph's* 'Willow Walks' competition to find Britain's Best Village Cricket Ground.

Joel's arrival was greeted by Wivey winning the toss. What followed Bugsy's gleeful hand-rubbing was, to be fair, a bit of an anti-climax.

To the immense relief of the sphincter clenching Bridgetown batters, farm lads ruddy faced and ruddy scared, scribbling their last wills and testaments on the backs of fag packets, Joel took no active part in the match. Instead, moments before the start of play, he smiled Bugsy the broadest of apologies and ambled along the main road in his size 15 boots a few hundred yards to the *Badger's Holt* pub.

He returned with six pints of ale on a tray. After shuffling carefully across the Exe spanning, narrow, helpfully railed, wooden footbridge that joined the road to the cricket pitch he whiled away a few hours of sunshine sat on a bench in the shade of a leafy chestnut tree, his back to the burbling river where cricket balls splashed, retrieved by paddling volunteers sharing a long poled fishing net, mallards cruised, and where stoic herons troutling-stabbed.

Locals still debate whether to place a new brass plaque saying, "A 'Big Bird' Supped Here" beside that screwed to the bench bearing the existing dedication:

"Silver Jubilee Queen Elizabeth II
1952-1977
Presented to
The villagers of Exton and Bridgetown
By the Women's Institute
Made by R.W.B from locally grown oak."

The 'Hero' of my chagrin similarly lacked any animated qualities. I speak of a bat misrepresented by branding and newly arrived from Hong Kong having been snapped up on eBay by Wivey's opener Derek for a quid at auction. But Caveat Emptor, 'let the buyer beware', as they say.

In the moments before poddling to the crease I wasn't beware of anything as I borrowed the bat off Derek in a determined effort to cement a place in Wivey 2nds.

The first ball I faced arrived waist high, very slowly and very wide down leg. Clenching teeth within a set jaw, I swung the wooden lump. 'Clunk'. The Hero had made contact with all the springiness one might expect from a weathered oak bench, and the ball looped gently, ever so gently, to a mightily surprised short backward square leg. The feared words of warning whirled in my head: "Lowest score carries the kit bag."

A quarter of a century ago a conciliatory gesture by my sportsmaster doubling as umpire, after I had taken three wickets against Blundell's School, reprieved me from such onerous undertaking. But there was no chance of redemption now. Not even by giving an extra tweak to my effort ball in my single over and bowling the rabbit wielding the willow middle stump, nor by my loud-mouthed yells of "HOWZAT! HOWZAT! HOWZAT! … I'M VINDICATED!" did I convince anybody.

"Well Chazzer, at least you talk a good game," Chris of my team said, before pointing at the smelly jumble of cricketing heaviness.

Oh yes, kit bags were a problem. And for the job of transporting them meant somebody had to be allocated. At Somerset Mervyn Kitchen recalled the responsibility fell on his friend Bill Alley. They played together and travelled together in an age when there were no sponsored cars as there are now.

"Everybody used to throw all our old kit bags into the back of Bill's Morris Oxford van," Mervyn told me. "Being yellow and black it was nicknamed 'The Wasp', and it used to buzz up the road and buzz back again.

We used to turn up at places at 12 o'clock or 1 o'clock at night. There were no motorways in those days. And going home I used to be there navigating, and nodding off after having been playing that day, and Bill would slap me hard on the leg with all the power he had. 'Kitchen sleeps when Alley sleeps and not before,' he used to say."

In the same way as Mervyn and Bill were inseparable as travelling companions so were Vic Marks and Peter Roebuck. A journey to Derbyshire, kit bags on the back seat, still sticks in their memory.

"We found Derby no trouble at all," said Peter. "Then we couldn't find the hotel. So we went round the main Derby ring road and asked a policeman. We followed his instructions to the best of our ability and continued going round the ring road and found the same policeman. So we asked him again. Off we set again around the circular. Eventually we found a policeman, but in a different position. Unfortunately it was the same policeman. On seeing us he announced that if we asked him for directions again he was going to arrest us."

But when it came to getting into travelling trouble Peter "Robbo' Robinson, an all-rounder and coach to the first team during the Glory Years, won the biscuit. Although it wasn't his fault that the transport involved had excess capacity after one of his 180 Somerset appearances.

I take you back to 1967 and the aftermath of the Lord's Gillette Cup final – the first time Somerset had ever got to such a big event. Robbo and other Somerset players, including Mervyn, had had the cheek to ask for a few more shillings as a result of getting there, only to be told: "Hang on a minute you've signed contracts that say you play any game the county wishes."

There had been tremendous weather, smocks, hay on the prongs of pitchforks, and barrels of cider. The balcony of the Kent dressing room was draped with hops. Unfortunately Somerset lost a low scoring game. And after it Somerset team members found a young supporter comatose in the gutter much the worse for scrumpy.

Robbo and others looked through his pockets and found that he lived in Taunton's Hamilton Road. Being a good Samaritan Robbo had the kind idea of bunging him on the team coach and taking him back to Taunton. This gained a unison of approval. Something positive would emerge from the disappointment of the day. However, on eventually delivering their ward back to Hamilton Road the thoughtful men of Somerset got a rocket from the lad's mother. The reason? The young chap was supposed to have been in London on his honeymoon.

Let it be said when travelling en masse even a simple anecdote, a getting of something off someone's chest, can quite put a team off its tea, not to mention distracting them altogether from the game of cricket.

This happened very recently as Wivey pootled by minibus, as fate would have it, to the annual game at Bridgetown. And it was something that caused me to reflect that getting to grounds on my mercenary tod was perhaps not a bad thing.

It had been a traumatised Grant, Wivey's lanky young talent of a batsman cum fast bowler, who needed 'to share', to break-up the convivial chitchat of Somerset's chances of winning the County Championship. But what may have been cathartic for him succeeded in only creating troubled minds within the rest of the team.

Grant's day job was that of an Social Services OAP 'stander-upper' – an OAP falls over, their personal alarm bleeps, Grant responds by arriving with an inflatable chair, and the fallen is blown upright. Simple. Unfortunately, twenty-four hours earlier Grant had been called too late. He arrived at the open doorway of scene just as the paramedics were doing the job of lifting an old man off the floor. Unfortunately the poor soul was in such a state of decomposition that he left his jellified face stuck to the floorboards.

Grant recounted the queasy bits in graphic detail. And the reaction aboard the minibus was mixed, ranging from the retchings of revulsion, hyperthyroid– eyes bulging out, to inappropriate nervous giggles.

All this was unbeknown to my wife and I loyally turning up to watch but with the game already underway. At first glance the nature at Bridgetown was nothing remarkable. A lone heron stood on one leg mid-stream like Ian Anderson at a Jethro Tull gig. A small flotilla of mallards floated where the river ran deep and languid below tangles of embedded bank tree roots. On the outfield yellowhammers coupled and swifts boomeranged while the purple flower heads of bugle ground hugged, hopeful of avoiding the crush of cricket boots. Joel's bench was occupied by a black labrador and a bloke flicking drunken wasps from his cider glass while a golden labrador preoccupied itself chasing the game – a cock pheasant. And Ernie and his wife, the most ardent of Wivey supporters, had ensconced themselves near a heap of grass clippings beside the riverbank having brought picnic chairs and a basket stuffed with yummies.

Then it slowly dawned on me that Wivey wasn't psychologically quite in the right mindset. There were small hints, like the odd dropped dolly catch, the seemingly lackadaisical attempts at outfield ball stopping, wicky Felix morphing into a human sieve, or Titch bowling four no-balls in an over off a three step 'run-up'. But when the rhythm's gone, it's gone. At least I thought, as a casual observer, as far as Titch was concerned matters hadn't reached the proportions of the thirteen-ball terror over bowled by Leicestershire's Scott Boswell at Marcus Trescothick during the C&G Trophy final in 2001. A 'promising' product of the Dennis Lillee's MRF Pace foundation, Scott sent down eight wides, five of them in a row. The Lord's slope and his own sweaty palms had been his undoing, breaking him as a man and prompting him to become a teacher.

For Wivey amid the green fields of the Exe Valley, even when balls were sent down Bridgetown's artificial strip there or thereabouts they came at great expense. Take Jake for instance, Grant's companion in the quick bowling stakes. Normally so laid back, he began to show the true measure of latent trauma as length and line dissolved.

Poor Jake delivered salvos of half-pitch buffet balls that were mercilessly walloped and tonked by Bridgetowners helping themselves with agricultural aplomb. Among them was Tom Carson, England's Under-21 hockey captain adjusting nicely to a change of discipline. Attempted yorkers arriving as full tosses met with the same fate. Distress became supplanted by anger, but with no change.

The solitary heron wisely heaved itself skywards with a lugubrious croak to seek safer waters. The mallard flotilla turning squadron soon followed, quacking noisily, fed up with bombardment from a ball repeatedly getting a soaking. As it bobbed along in the Exe current, paddlers, taking turns with the long-poled fishing net, splashed and scooped while slipping and cursing on stones for the better part of half an hour.

About the only time the net wasn't needed the sodden ball had sailed over both river and main road to thump halfway up an impressively sheer rock face, dislodging bracken fern, and sending sedimentary shrapnel down onto tarmac, a passing Volvo estate and a touring caravan before the rolling ball was run over by a tractor. Tea came as a respite for all, apart from Jake. He spent the best part of ten minutes red-faced, sweating his nuts off doing press-ups by the pavilion steps.

Post tea things got worse for Wivey come their turn to bat. Beyond the wire fence abutting the paint of the boundary line pavilion side where foxgloves drooped, it was sheep, not Wivey that had got the runs. Jake's dad Derek, once described as "the best fly-half outside Bath and Bristol of all time", by taking his keen eye off a forward defensive due to the flight path of a wasp, started the rot.

Dennis, having been joined by Grant, and normally so decisive at the crease, pushed off for a single, calling as he did so "Yes-yes, one – no-no-no-NO. Oh f-f-f-f." In the nick he time he remembered the decorum of captaincy over impressionable youth. "FUDGE!"

"BAA," replied a boundary sheep.

Only Matty, Wivey's 'Mister Dependable', saved the blushes, hitting 8 sixes while reportedly wearing a spangly G-string. From the rest, my lad Felix included, resistance was light and a heavy defeat was inevitable. Several hands would be carrying the kit bag, apart from the unfortunate collapsing with testicular torsion. Although he seemed to recover a little after being offered a left over sandwich.

"Should've kept the story to myself," bemoaned Grant as he leaned, skulking, a volunteer to fishing net duty, on the river boundary rail.

"Oh never mind, what's out is out, And in medical parlance: What's dead is dead. The only suffering toady is Wivey's," I consoled, and received an elbow from my wife as, en masse, Bridgetown were in the mood for celebration.

"Going up the Badger's?" the groundsman to Bridgetown's artificial wicket asked Bugsy in an attempt to mitigate whatever might have been amiss.

"Do one-legged ducks swim round in circles?" replied Bugsy, suddenly miraculously cheered.

A few days later I learnt that one of Joel Garner's buckskin cricket boots described as a "gurt big'un", signed by Joel and in the Somerset Cricket Museum, had been chosen as an item to represent Somerset as part of a major new project for the *BBC - A History of the World*. Other items included a Bath Chair and the Laughing Sailor.

One of the remits was to make the item interesting and give an unexpected story. Stephen Minnit, the chap in charge of Somerset County Museum, helped to choose the objects for the county. "The idea is to use objects, initially museum objects that have both local resonance and a much wider one, world-wide or other parts of the world," he said. "It's just a way of getting away from the usual history book or perhaps just looking at artefacts in a museum from a local perspective and put things in a wider way and gain a different insight into world history."

Well, perhaps the most interesting piece of history attached to Joel's boot was that it was worn on the day Somerset clinched the John Player League title in 1979 by beating Nottingham, Derek Randall and Clive Rice et al, at Trent Bridge. The other boot 'disappeared' after falling off the players' balcony, snaffled up by a member of the ecstatic crowd of Somerset supporters below.

And as stories went my son Felix loved the story about Joel's afternoon at Bridgetown. So he did 'a Bugsy' on Somerset's Max Waller.

"What? Play for Wivey? I'll have to get back to you on that one," Max had responded rather too hastily. "I'll take that as a no, then," said Felix.

The Match Where Joel Garner Lost His Gurt Big'un

NOTTINGHAMSHIRE v SOMERSET

John Player League 1979
Trent Bridge, Nottingham on 9 September 1979 (40-over match)
Nottinghamshire won the toss and decided to field
Umpires: R Julian and J van Geloven

Somerset innings

*BC Rose		b Watson	4
PW Denning		b Rice	21
IVA Richards		b Hemmings	25
PM Roebuck	c Birch	b Watson	50
IT Botham	c Birch	b Hemmings	30
GI Burgess		b Bore	6
VJ Marks	c Randall	b Cooper	14
J Garner	c and	b Rice	0
D Breakwell		not out	8
CH Dredge		not out	2
Extras (8 b, 15 lb, 2 nb)			25
Total (8 wickets, innings closed, 39 overs)			185

Did not bat +DJS Taylor

Fall of wickets: 1-10, 2-56, 3-58, 4-114, 5-131, 6-166, 7-168, 8-182

Nottinghamshire bowling: Watson: 8-0-27-2, Bore: 8-2-18-1, Hemmings: 8-0-43-2, Cooper: 7-0-55-1, Rice: 7-2-13-2, Tunnicliffe: 1-0-4-0

Nottinghamshire innings

SB Hassan	c Taylor	b Botham	6
RT Robinson		run out	35
DW Randall	c Taylor	b Garner	1
*CEB Rice		lbw b Dredge	39
JD Birch		lbw b Dredge	2
HT Tunnicliffe	c Taylor	b Burgess	5
+MJ Harris		not out	17
EE Hemmings		b Richards	0
WK Watson	c Taylor	b Garner	5
KE Cooper		b Garner	0
MK Bore		lbw b Botham	7
Extras (5 lb, 4 nb, 3 w)			12
Total (all out, 33.1 overs)			129

Fall of wickets: 1-11, 2-15, 3-83, 4-91, 5-91, 6-99, 7-102, 8-119, 9-119, 10-129

Somerset bowling: Garner: 6-2-16-3, Botham: 5.1-0-18-2, Dredge: 8-0-28-2, Burgess: 7-0-40-1, Richards: 7-1-15-1

Somerset won by 56 runs and so won the John Player League Title 1979.

A Duck Tale

Sammy Woods told the following story to his good friend Major CHB Pridham:

"I used to take what I called my Farmers X to play matches in the different towns of Somerset and Devon, and what a good time we had! I generally had the assistance of Robson, Tyler, and Braund. Sometimes I would have five or six farmers. Still, we generally won our games, and would finish the day with dinner and sing-song. One day I had three farmers playing for me, all of them about 6 feet 3 inches tall. Just before the game started, three white ducks crossed he wicket. I remarked to them it was a bad omen. They didn't understand why until – I having put them in 1, 2 and 3 – they all got bowled out first ball. I had the ducks killed, and placed one in each of their bags. As they didn't have cricket bags, but hand-bags, I hope they found them that evening or next morning. I never inquired!"

Team Kit Bag

A cricket bag's a splendid thing for any team to own,
Exuding possibilities and pure testosterone.
Famous victories, golden moments, feats with bat & ball,
Humiliation, ecstasy, the bag has shared them all.
We never even loiter when the skipper wants to lift it;
It takes a pair of supermen to pick it up & shift it.
It's not that we're unhelpful, selfish or chicken hearted;
We just don't want to bust a gut before the match has started.

Arthur Salway

NINE

Of Boaters and Icebreakers

"There is a widely held and quite erroneous
belief that cricket is just another game."
HRH The Duke of Edinburgh.

Boaters are not just those men who once rowed about the Tone fishing out exuberantly struck cricket balls with a net, they are also sennit straw headwear affectionately known as 'somers' particularly favoured by Harrovians.

A family heirloom from my Grandfather's day, a Victorian team photograph of fulsome moustaches, stripy shirts and blazers captured in front of Taunton's wooden pavilion, I'm reliably told, in 1891 before a match between Somerset and Middlesex, hung in my hallway between the key hooks and a striking picture of the cat. Amongst the twelve bods wearing caps that included Sammy Woods, the Palariet brothers and the self-satisfied looking captain Herbert Tremenheere Hewett, are three wearing boaters, one of which I haven't a clue who it is. The other two, I understood, were really quite important.

Dark, bushy, spade-bearded due to being unable to tie his bow or cravat following an arm injury sustained when his horse shied up on being spooked by a steamroller, Henry Murray Anderson, one of the giants in the story of Somerset cricket, is seen standing stiff and immaculate. Peter Roebuck clarions Henry huge credit in *From Sammy to Jimmy* for giving Somerset "unstinting service" for nearly forty years, paying debts and building "a fine club". Henry in turn kept a picture of his beloved Somerset team in the bathroom of his Henlade home, possibly to keep reminding himself of what he got himself into.

Seated middle-for-diddle the other recognisable 'somered' fellow is a large nosed, white whiskered gentleman leaning on a thin, expensive looking cane who happened to live in the most beautiful house in England. Or so Auberon Waugh thought.

The white-whiskered gentleman was the autocratic Sir Spenser Ponsonby-Fane, the chap who had brought the treaty that ended the Crimean War back from Paris and who had inherited Brympton D'Evercy. At the time of the photograph he was in his sixties and in his first year as President of the club. As a man of public stature he sat for Walter Ouless RA, regarded as an "impressive exponent of character" and the artist that painted Charles Darwin, the controversial, extremely white whiskered chap of *On the Origin of the Species* notoriety. And whereas the Darwin likeness hangs in Christ's College at Cambridge University, fittingly, Sir Spenser's portrait ended up in the long room of the Lord's Pavilion.

In his younger days he mostly played for Surrey. *Scores and Biographies* described him as "A free and lively hitter, forward and to leg. Also a good field, generally long-leg, middle wicket or point. Is remarkably quick between wickets, but has run himself and partner out very frequently." This is what maybe gave him the credentials to dabble in politics rather than aspire to become, say, a judge.

And although he was private secretary to Lord Palmerston and Attaché at Washington, cricket was his first love. It's not for me to suggest otherwise. I'm sure I could be persuaded that his fathering of eleven children was no more than a veritable attempt to derive a complete cricket team from his own loins. Not a bad notion seeing that Brympton had its own pitch. However, by the age of twenty-one Sir Spenser had already been committed to playing away.

On Independence Day evening 1845, over a dinner at the Blenheim Hotel in London's Bond Street, after a match that afternoon against Harrow School, Sir Spenser together with his brother Frederick and their friends John Loraine Baldwin and Richard Penruddocke Long, former Harrovians to a man, there and then decided to form a nomadic cricket team. It seemed a good wheeze to promote the good spirit of amateur cricket. But the question was: Under what name? Something a touch romantic, perhaps. Maybe 'The Gypsies'? No, that was too plebeian for those of noble birth. Ah, but give the gypsies a classical twist by using the Italian 'I Zingari', now that would do nicely. Next up they framed rules which were half-serious and half-comic such as "the Entrance fee be nothing" and "the Annual Subscription do not exceed the

Entrance" and many of them survive today, including the decree to "keep your promise", "keep your temper" and "keep your wicket up".

And come daylight the following morning they informed William Boland, "a barrister with an extensive practice and a formidable presence", that he was Perpetual President and twenty of their friends that they were now Zingaros, members.

The affirmation of amateurism was vital, mainly because most sides in those days employed professionals or given men, to bolster them, whereas the Zingaros preferred to do without one.

After much consideration black, red and gold were chosen as club colours, the representation of "out of darkness, through fire, into light". The colours attracted attention in cricketing circles, so much so that they were 'appropriated' by the Marylebone Cricket Club who kept to the red and gold and left out the black thus creating the famous egg and bacon effect tie.

Elitist, patronised by royalty, acknowledged in high society and careful whom they chose to play for them, I Zingari were very soon able to turn out a side strong enough to hold its own against any professional eleven. In 1877 they beat Yorkshire at the Scarborough Festival and in 1882 and 1884 they had a fixture against the touring Australians. Uniquely for an amateur club, Wisden reported all of its matches since 1867, although ceased to do so in 2005. And today the Somerset Cricket Museum that houses a remarkable collection of I Zingari memorabilia originally assembled at Brympton continues its close association with the famous itinerants by having Charles Clive Ponsonby-Fane, Sir Spenser's great great grandson, as its patron.

So really it goes without saying that I Zingari is the oldest and perhaps most illustrious of nomadic clubs, but of course there are others that have earned respect, such as Free Foresters, Incogniti, Arabs, that claim Sir Ian Botham as their president, and Cryptics, that incidentally happen to be 100 years 'not out' as I keypad tap this. However, the one truly worthy of raising eyebrows, purely due to noteworthy achievement, especially since they've only been around since Sir Beefy's benefit year in 1984, has to be the touring team that frequently visit Somerset, the Chelsea Arts Club Cricket Club. And more often than not they meet with success.

A visit to Rode, out on the Wiltshire borderland, comes first. Here the visitors invariably play through hosings of rain. It's a village that's damp at the best of times. One of mill ponds and steams where the dye Royal Blue was invented by the village millers. And which, long after a photograph taken in 1895 of the village cricket team showing-off several pairs of braces, six flat caps and a bowler hat, as well as a singular boater, has also become a home to sporting excellence of the non-cricketing variety, namely the England rugby captain Lewis 'Mad Dog' Moody MBE. However, as yet the local cricket club has been unable to persuade that hero of England's 2003 Rugby World Cup victory, and now of Bath Rugby, to apply his renowned physical commitment to the summer game, even simply as a blonde instrument of intimidation growling at silly mid-on.

But although Rode may have had a large attraction, top of the Chelsea Arts Club's Somerset itinerary is their match at North Perrott against a local eleven calling themselves Merriott House. Hired for the day, as grounds go in Somerset, picturesque Willis Lane is rather a grand one, particularly with regard to the magnificent, two-storey balconied and lattice-windowed pavilion that was opened in 2000 by Vic Marks, not to mention having a smart scorer's hut and electronic scoreboard. North Perrott itself has played at Willis Lane as a club since 1946 courtesy of the Hoskyns, a wealthy family founded on girtweb making – which it's said was something to do with sail making rather than anything largely Aracnid. Then thanks to a generous anonymous sponsor and a Sports and Arts Foundation grant the club bought the ground off the said family in the 1990s.

However, North Perrott and Merriott House are not the only teams to exhibit their skills at Willis Lane and it's a surface the Chelsea Arts Club to a man get quite excited about the prospect of playing on.

With Somerset sometimes using the ground for practice sessions there are thoughts of treading on hallowed ground once trod by Sir Ian and Sir Viv before thoughts turn to maidens. That's to say illustrious Somerset ladies like the Netherland's Izzy Westbury and England's Anya Shrubsole. And of course Fran Wilson, a lass who incidentally claims to base her batting on Marcus Trescothick and that expensive short term import Ricky 'Punter' Ponting who graced Somerset with his presence for a month in 2004. During that time he pulled the flagging county team up by its bootstraps before departing with an average of 99.00. Fran could have done worse than have Punter as a role model when she takes the field at Willis Lane, a ground that has become a godsend. With the Somerset women's cricket team having no fixed home it has recently played half its home fixtures here.

In the light of this, the Chelsea Arts Club, despite the excellent Somerset tea during which large pieces of delicious cake, egg mayo sandwiches, cans of ale, etcetera, were consumed, could be considered lightweights; especially so given that other fixtures include matches against Grannies and Butterflies. Yet the club had sprung the odd surprise of major proportions.

Although in cricketing parlance, Maddocks, Kulasingam and 'Timble-Tumble' the Magician may not have the kudos of Kieswetter, Collingwood and Broad, or indeed Lewis Moody, these Chelsea chaps arrived in Somerset as World Champions. Straight up. They had won a cricket World Cup for England.

And their achievement was right up there with another touring club team, Devon and Somerset Wanderers. Those Englishmen went on a jolly to France and returned with the Olympic cricket title – a title, which as a result, Great Britain still holds today.

> "Exposition Universelle 1900
> Match de Cricket
> France contre Angleterre
> Dimanche 19 et Lundi 30 Aout
> Velodrome de Vincennes,"

declared a handbill advertising the game making no mention of the word 'Olympic'.

While in Paris the Devon and Somerset Wanderers had entered 'a competition' on a whim, called themselves Great Britain, and joined the three other teams that had already put their names forward, Belgium, Holland and France. Bizarrely, none of sides seemed aware that they were taking part in the Olympics. However, Belgium and Holland pulled out, leaving only Great Britain v. France. Oddly, the French team consisted of Britons living in Paris, reportedly mostly members of the British Embassy. A contemporary journalist described the French themselves as "too excitable to enjoy the game," and added, "No Frenchman could be persuaded to play more than once. A cricketer in France is a stranger in a strange land looked upon with mingled awe and contempt by the average Frenchman."

The two-day 'international' took place inside a 20,000-seater banked cycling track. The crowd consisted of a dozen or so bemused gendarmes. To possibly swell numbers the cricket captains agreed to a 12-a-side game. Potential spectators had hardly been encouraged by an explanation in *La Vie Au Grand Air*, the official publication of the Games, which described cricket as "this sport without colour to the uninitiated".

The Wanderers batted first and scored a creditable 117. France were then bowled out for 78. The Wanderers scored 145 for 5 second time around setting the hosts a target of 185. In the event, this proved way beyond them, and they were bowled out for a meagre 26. The English side, that's to say the Wanderers, were awarded silver medals, the 'French' bronze ones – both XIIs also received miniature replicas of the 11-year-old Eiffel Tower.

In the Wanderers team, and their second innings top scorer with 59, was one Alfred Bowerman. Born in Haygrove, Bridgwater before moving to Broom-field, Alfred was a middle-order batsman who played twice for Somerset with absolutely no success. He was a non-event.

Whereas the English team's journey back to the hotel was eventful to say the least. The driver of one of the two coaches had become rather caught up in the day's events and having guddled himself senseless was driven back inside his own carriage. The other, apparently in a similar state, crashed his coach, causing bandages to be needed for some of the passengers whose boaters got grubby in the street.

And so ended the competition. The match was only retrospectively formally recognised as being an Olympic contest in 1912, when the International Olympic Committee met to compile the definitive list of all events in the five modern Olympiads up to that point. By the time of the St Louis Games in 1904 cricket had been forgotten. The newspapers at home completely ignored the match

The word on the grave-vine emerging from Taunton's County Stores was that there were imminent plans afoot to re-enact that great Olympic triumph in 2012 while the London Games were on. The emporium's owner Hugh Duder, for his sins President of the Somerset Stragglers, was most surely in the know. By all accounts the nostalgic notion was a Blundell's public school thing. A jolly old boys wheeze. Former Blundellian Vic Marks would be proud. But facing tough economic times there would be no need to take the Eurostar to Paris. As a rematch venue, Castle Carey could suffice as the place to alight. The reason? Five of the victorious Wanderers had played for the town's cricket club, and 2012 would be the club's 175th anniversary. So no commem-orative Eiffel towers were planned. Being Castle Carey perhaps an alternative would be to present locally weaved horsehair mats.

Understandably the media have been much more interested in the accom-plishment of the Chelsea Art Club when they won the World title of the variant of the game that's played on ice.

And let it be said, this nothing to do with Torville or Deane, nor indeed any tomfool knockabout victory gained in the snows of April that happened to welcome the start of the English cricket season when the real cricketers hug radiators and leather lies sodden in the slush. And nor was it to do with the days when George Lambert, a well-known Gloucestershire bowler, had come to Somerset as a coach. Memories still linger when, at the start of a season, he had sent the Somerset squad out to the army camp at Norton Fitzwarren. There, in a white wonderland, a great big PTI instructor who was about fifteen stone and built like a battleship, had the squad all running across country, carrying packs on their backs, and lifting rifles up and down.

The Chelsea Arts Club had no need of such rigorous training when they relied so much on lady luck and a bit of sense in a place considerably more forbidding than Taunton Deane. In 2006 the club won Ice Cricket World Cup in Estonia with a sensible bright orange ball of composite plastic that was easy to find in a snowdrift.

Despite the surreal of the occasional, and potentially off-putting, windsurfer gliding past the ice wicket powered by coloured sail, and many a pirouetting skater, the Chelsea Arts Cricket Club won the title fair and square slipping and sliding upon Harku boating lake in the city of Tallinn. Fur hats and numb fingers were the order of the day in harsh temperatures ranging between minus 10 to minus 25.

A Union Jack was lost to the wind and entangled itself in a tree as the team rounded things off nicely with a celebratory dip through an ice hole. While from a tinny CD player came the immortal verse:

> "I will not cease from Mental Fight,
> Nor shall my Sword sleep in my hand:
> Till we have built Jerusalem
> In England's green and pleasant Land."

Never could the hymn *Jerusalem* with its words by William Blake and music written by Sir Hubert Parry have sounded so incongruous.

The media attention that followed English World Cup glory was significant, gaining airtime both on the BBC's Breakfast programme and Sky News. Indeed, Reuters syndicated the story and video footage worldwide. There were soundbites amid the frostbite such as: "It's a bit mad and it's extremely cold." "I would not recommend it for the feeble or the weak," I tried to bowl slow but the icy blast blew the ball back to me," and "You think you have the ball and it isn't there, it just goes through your fingers." Added to this, such a high profile brought sponsorship to the chilly tournament from a cider company, though it was not one from Somerset. Hereford's Bulmers, now owned by the giant Australian brewers Foster's, had got in on the act.

However, given their versatility of adapting to conditions it's hardly surprising that the Chelsea Arts Club Cricket Club can adjust to regular success on their annual Somerset travels.

The Rules of Ice Cricket

Teams can have a maximum of 10 players and a minimum of 6.

Wides count as two extra runs with no extra ball, with leniency given to the bowler as he finds it tough standing up most of the time.

If you hit either a wild Moose or a cross-country skier, an extra 6 runs is added to your score.

The boundaries are either snow-banks or are patrolled by officials on ice skates. If you strike a skater an extra 6 runs is added to your score.

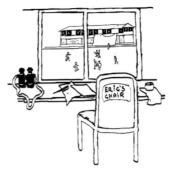

Of Inkwells and Rebels

"My secret arsenal is an infinite, ageless inkwell."
Brandon Boyd (American musician and artist).

While Charlie Sedgebeer tended to draw attention to himself as he sold smudgable scorecards whiffing of fresh ink by wearing his wartime medals pinned to his white uniform, that modest man of gentle humour, Eric Hill, tucked away his DFC and DFM for courage in a drawer somewhere and preferred to be less conspicuous. The press box had been Eric's second home ever since Somerset had released him as a player in 1951 and he had pottered seamlessly into local journalism and then outward to the *Daily Telegraph*.

Sadly, within the month of July, as Somerset limbered up at Taunton to take on Northants in their 2010 Twenty20 Quarter final, there was news from the Quantock foothills – Eric had passed away in Williton hospital and the club had sent 'sincere condolences' to Dorothy, his widow.

Ever since he was a small boy, and his Dad had run up a Somerset flag in the family-run sweet shop each time the county won a game, a passion for Somerset cricket had entered Eric's blood. It was further ingrained while as a pupil at Taunton School, and never left him.

The only time that he was distracted from the game was during the Second World War when, as an observer attached to 544 squadron in Oxfordshire, he flew low level photo reconnaissance sorties into France, Scandinavia, East Germany and Poland; stuff that made more him hassled than an easyJet steward. Then, after the War's end and mentored by Arthur Wellard, he played as a professional, a chap playing for money; something that in the pre-war years would have been frowned upon. Yes, it was tolerated, but scarcely encouraged in man of pedigree. But on debut Eric, a tall right hand opening batsman, had earned his money's worth – helping Somerset record a one wicket victory at Lord's in May 1947 against a star studded Middlesex side that included Bill Edrich and Denis Compton. He went on play 72 first class matches for Somerset in which he scored 2118 runs, with a best of 85 against Northants at Kettering.

But it really went without saying that Eric was as modest of his contributions to his beloved Somerset as, like the majority of others of his generation, he had been self-effacing about his wartime exploits. And bravery first shown while flying around in the likes of the 'wooden wonder', the twin-propped de Havilland Mosquito extended to repeatedly climbing the ladder up to that other wooden wonder, Taunton's wooden, white painted press box, perceived by many as precarious as a pigeon's nest since it was first nailed together in 1890 above the old pavilion.

And the box was where on a damp, chilly one-dayer in the Axa Equity and Law League Vic Marks and I went to catch up with Eric, wrapped up warm in a thick cardigan and wind-cheater, not much more than a hundred years later. The match reduced by May downpours had been 'squidged in' having been scheduled for the 'off' day during the Championship game between the two counties that had seen Bristolian Paul Bird make his first class debut.

By way of Somerset captain, the effete-seeming figure of entrenchment, Chris Tavare having retired Andy Hayhurst had taken the helm to lead the likes of A Payne, N A Folland, Taunton born HRJ Trump, Bridgwater's finest, RJ Harden, and "Trooster' the tall, fiery Dutch fast bowler, Andre van Troost. It had to be said that Andy's appointment had only been after a scratch around the club and a few grumbles behind his back. He had been third choice after failed attempts to attract Derbyshire's John Morris, infamous for flying a Tiger Moth biplane with David Gower over Carrara during an England warm-up match against Queensland, and Leicestershire's James Whitaker, famous in 1986 for having bones broken in both hands by Malcolm Marshall.

With Andy's cohorts in the field after a particularly dismal collective batting display in which he had second top scored with 28, I'm sure I wasn't the only one rueing that Trooster wasn't playing that day. His deliveries of rapidity would induce Mark Butcher to later reminisce on Test Match Special that the Dutchman made Waqar Younis look like "a medium pacer". Anyway, things where very quiet in the River Stand without the customary smattering of "cock-a-doodle-doos" reserved for Trooster from that particular corner of the ground.

Vic and I entered the box as a cheer arose from the spectators, and Eric began penning some quick words with a biro. There had been a sudden departure for a familiar Warwickshire batter, 'The Prince of Port of Spain'. Although in retrospect he might have been saving himself for exertions required the following month when his mammoth 501 not out against Durham at Edgbaston became the record for the highest individual score in first-class cricket.

"Brian Lara's out for 11! Paul Bird just bowled him, his first wicket. Through the blooming gate. Must have swung and kept low. Wonderful for the new lad," said a beaming Eric turning to us.

"Really? Are you sure?" Vic couldn't feign mighty surprise that Somerset's latest right-arm fast-medium prospect was exceeding expectations.

"Perhaps the ball hit a puddle," I interjected helpfully, and was rightfully ignored.

Then a thought seemed to cross Vic's mind. "Do you remember Stuart Symington causing carnage?" he asked impishly, obviously to nudge a good story from Eric for my enlightenment.

Eric glanced out of the press box window at Paul Bird running in to bowl again with a bounce in his lope, and gave a chuckle. "Yep, 1948. We were playing Leicestershire here at Taunton and Harold Gimblett and I opened together. Symington was their new amateur opening bowler. He wasn't very good really, but a nice enough chap. And he got both of us out for 20 odd, which was ridiculous. Sort of holing out at mid-on and mid-off.

"Gimblett was furious. And he said, 'I'm going to murder that bloke in the second innings'. I said, 'Take it easy'. However, Gimmo was pretty well true to his word. When Symington pitched it up Gimmo hit it straight back over his head, and when he dropped it short it went many a mile. I gave it a bit of stick, too – a couple of singles down to third man.

"After three or four overs Symington stood in the middle of the pitch and exclaimed, 'God, if this is first class cricket I've had it!' Gimmo responded with, 'Thank your lucky stars Charlie Barnett's given up, mate'."

This latter reference was to Gloucestershire's middle order stalwart who although having had a reputation for being a tad vulnerable to early dismissal had walloped eleven sixes in an innings of 194 against Somerset in 1934.

But as if to proving the theory of where there's life there's hope, Symington went on to captain Leicestershire a year after Gimblett's thrash.

However, it was doubtful Paul Bird would attain such rapid status, as, after a series of closely spaced four-balls had thumped into the boundary boards, he was replaced by Somerset's glimmer of light from the Punjab, Mushtaq Ahmed. His googlies though seemed to cause little trouble to the others that remained in Warwickshire's top order. Willow continued to contact forcibly with leather.

Yet, in the world of surprises that had brought Lara's wicket there was also undisguised incredulity that the ancient press box had survived the Taylor Report. Vic's eyes gave it away as he surveyed the lofty confines.

Eric concurred with Vic's amazement. The thing was, the report had condemned the main stand. Quite frankly, this puzzled Eric a bit. He assumed they would condemn the press box at the same time as it was nearly falling down anyway, and especially as one of the two conventional doors was "rather hard" to open and the unconventional, a trap door escape route, lay hidden away under a thin, cheap carpet.

"Best they covered it over," said Eric. "Dear old Ron Roberts, a journalist working for what seemed like 'forty-three' papers fell down it trying to get to the telephones in a hurry."

"What?" I said. "The rebellious Ron Roberts of 1953 fame."

"Umm," muttered Eric almost inaudibly, "the very same."

Sustained failure in the late forties to the turn of the decade was too much to bear for even the most romantic of supporters. The inability of the team to even manage to compete led to a cussedly rebellious streak in Somerset's rank and file, and that included Eric.

Perhaps it was the sight of Arthur Wellard stumbling around Weston Festival with his shoelaces undone as an act of dissent to a committee he considered ignorant of cricketing matters and downright feeble in its appointment of incompetent captains and inept, talentless professionals

Come 1953 and enough was enough for Eric, and he became a 'troublemaker'. Together with Ron, and another journo, Bob Moore, Eric formed a bridgehead of rebel supporters to challenge the authority of the club committee. After much shenanigans, venomous argument, meetings in Taunton and Weston-super-Mare, complacency was shattered and frustration given expression. Within four seasons Somerset had finished third in the championship. Rebellion had led to rebirth. Well, for little a while at least.

As a flock of seagulls circled the ground and one or two landed in the outfield, Eric emitted an 'ooo-er'. Paul Bird was back on. Despite him being no 'Big Bird' a particularly nasty snorter from him had passed within a cat's whisker of Dermot Reeve's shnozzle. Twenty-four months beyond that and Dermot would move to Somerset as coach.

Back in his seat in the Taunton press box Eric quoted aloud from John Arlott's poetic phraseology, "the seagulls standing in line like vultures for Lillee". However, instead of the raucous call of gulls, the most audible sound was the bickering of sparrows.

Seeing Eric reach again for his biro that lay on the formica work top, Vic said, "John Arlott loved the old school desks with their holes for ink wells that used to be in here, didn't he?"

"He was *most* impressed by them, and used to bring up his friends to show them the inkwells. At the time of the 'reburbishment' I even remarked to Ken Jones, who had been reporting from the box longer than I had, 'let's save one of those little inkwells and we can get it off to John'. Later when I raised the matter again Ken was embarrassed to say that when they took the place apart everything fell to bits. Umm."

Locally, Eric is even more missed than John. "Eric was like the wallpaper on the wall," Mervyn Kitchen had told me as he recalled walking onto the field to umpire a Durham game at Taunton. "I put the bails on and looked around to see if Eric was in his familiar place in the old press box. He acknowledged me and I doffed my hat to him and the game proceeded. Eric's been there since God knows how long."

By September 2010 and the Clydesdale Bank semi-final encounter with Essex, and with Alison Mitchell of the new generation of BBC commentators having had a whinge about having to climb the press box ladder and what it would do to her hairdo, Richard, one of the safety stewards, glanced upwards from beneath the brim of his floppy sun hat and mused wistfully, "I'm sure Eric's still in there, you know".

"Without a doubt," I agreed, before asking if he remembered Paul Bird.

After a quizzical look from Richard I gave a prompt. "1994?"

Given a further moment or two's thought Richard replied, "Didn't he only ever play a couple of games in those bad old days? One more than, erm,

Bradleigh Donelan. Scrawny lad with lanky hair who I remember getting the Yorkshire skipper David Byas out"

"Maybe he did, but young Bird bowled Lara.

"Did he, by God."

"Pity he didn't go on to be as successful as Stuart Symington."

"You what?"

"Doesn't matter," I said.

But what of Paul Bird? Well, a bit of research showed that nowadays he was either turning out for Bath 4ths or Claverham (Yatton) Cricket Club.

On the other hand, Bradleigh Donelan is now a manager of an under-7s rugby team in the North West. Cricket for him is now something of the past, and his highlight came about even before his one match outing for Somerset.

The very first wicket to fall to his brand of off-spin was that of Sir Ian Botham. And it happened three years after the infamous 'Battle of Shepton Mallet' that saw a motion of no confidence in the Somerset Committee instigated by rebel members defeated by 1,828 votes to 798.

The *Daily Mail* reported "a last goodbye for Viv and Joel ... delivered by Cambridge Blue Nigel Popplewell. The Somerset rebels knew they were stumped the moment Popplewell stood before a crowd of 3,000 and revealed what life was like in a dressing room with three superstars. During a coura-geous two minutes in the 'witness box' the county's former opening batsman demolished an 11-week campaign for the reinstatement of Viv Richards and Joel Garner with an attack that ensured a 70 per cent confirmation of their sacking. 'Popplewell's speech was the killer,' said one of the rebel leaders before all the votes had been counted. 'Until then we thought we were in with a fighting chance. There was no pulling it round after that.'"

The upshot meant that the Committee's sacking of Sir Viv and Joel in prefer-ence for the Kiwi Martin Crowe was rubber-stamped. Sir Ian left Somerset in principled protest taking his presence elsewhere.

Consequently, Bradleigh continues to talk about his big moment at Hove. The record book reads: Worcestershire first innings – IT Botham bowled Donelan 8, Worcestershire second innings - IT Botham caught CM Wells bowled Donelan 4.

In an interview with the *Liverpool Daily Post* Bradleigh recalled: "I was just a young lad on the MCC groundstaff and was asked to play for Sussex seconds as a trial in 1989. As part of the trial I made my first team debut against Worcester. They threw me the ball to have a go but weren't really expecting much as I was a young lad against Botham, but I was a cocky Cockney and saw it as a great challenge for me. He went back to cut me and the ball went on to hit his off stump. Someone in the ground got a picture of it, while it was also the first ball my dad saw me bowl in county cricket. All in all it was a perfect day and I ended up with three wickets for 60 runs. Then in the night after the game, Beefy bought me a pint to say well done. It was brilliant."

The rebel in Eric might have thought it brilliant, too.

ELEVEN

Stretched Fingers and Chains

"Each well-known feature we espy:
The turf so grateful to the eye,
The Players dressed in flannels white,
And Umpires hailed with great delight."

Anon.

"**U**mpires need to be well-balanced men to survive, utterly certain of their sanity," Peter Roebuck opined. However, there's no doubting umpires can get away with blue bloody murder from the moment they pronounce "Play". Fact. Rule number one is that to undermine the white-coated one's authority just isn't cricket. Back in the good old days Richie Benaud was prone to the occasional harrumph followed by "I'll leave you to make your own minds up about that one".

With an umpire's life being so iffy euphemism will have its day when bluntness could otherwise lead to blows. Being 'adjudged ell bee', for example, can be translated as meaning 'the nut' was missing leg stump by a margin that endangered the square-leg umpire. Or 'given out' is a gift-wrapped decision deserving of thank-you letters from the fielding side. The integrity of genuine mistake can be tempered by pity, by panic or by those guesstimates after having been otherwise distracted. One is reluctant to add to this list psychological bullying – in which case the umpire must weigh up, without too much hesitation, whom he will least upset as post game post mortems at the bar can prove problematic dissections should he not have a 2-litre turbo for a quick getaway.

However, the rural image of the Somerset umpire is generally that of an affable and affectionate soul, the pockets of his white coat so often full of gubbins. This is especially true of a coat that is, more often than not, borrowed.

I speak from experience having volunteered to officiate at an under-13s encounter between Watchet and Wivey at Watchet's Memorial Ground.

To begin with I was full of the nostalgia that this was where Harold Gimblett once dominated proceedings. And here until recently Merv Parson umpired well into his eighties. Cricket was his life. Well, that and skittles. Often declaring "Och, there's lot of talent around here", he was nicknamed 'Watchit' on account of his infamy for giving hosts of ell bees.

However, nowadays although one side of the Watchet ground offers the tended shrubs of the urban park as Harold might have recognised them, the boundary edge shelter at the other lacks a degree of charm.

Such was the way of modern times, I thought, before donning the white coat and finding its pockets a tad bulky. Instinctively I had a rummage. Most of the things were explainable, like the broken pencil stub, the paper scrap, the six gravel stones, the several pellets of dried chewing gum, the two sticky, fluff-covered peppermint humbugs, and the four white feathers. What were not so explainable were the bits of shiny tin foil and the remnants of spliffs, those carefully made roll-ups that whiff of illicit substances.

The game got of to a conventional start with two teams more of less attired in whites. And I thought the keen home team lad admirable in gamely chasing a leg swoosh to in front of the shelter. Once there he stooped down twice before returning towards the wicket with the ball in one hand and what looked remarkably like a charred spliff stub in the other. With the lad being quicker getting rid of the ball, I was forced into making the same unpopular decision as those that had gone before me, confiscation.

On broaching the subject of the 'treasure' with the other umpire, a local in the know, it was illuminating to discover the shelter was where the town's druggies had the habit of hanging out.

However, one has to persevere with today's youth. The incoming of young blood is a necessity for grassroots strength and depth, even if terms that can be loosely applied – just look around the playing pool of any village club. The impetuosity of youth offsets the due caution and wariness of those bearing the wisdom lines of age. Obvious really.

But is such a quality as youth required for captaincy? This is the burning question asked ever more frequently by oldsters making way for the young bloods. Those perhaps of belly and many a wrinkle in their fifties, sixties, and even seventies, suffer hurt feelings having to kowtow to teenage leadership. Outwardly, news of displacement is taken philosophically. "S'pose you've got to let the youngsters have an opportunity," is a phrase begrudgingly uttered to those of sympathetic ear, when all the time they might silently swear: "Bloody sprogs". Then the thought can arise as to how to get one's own back. It was simple. One could don the white coat of the umpire. Or was I being too cynical?

I can only report my own dilemma when recruited as a non-bowling mercenary to wield the willow at number 11 for Lydeard St Lawrence 2nds and to be a 'shift' umpire. As the sun turned skin the colour of a boiled lobsters I had admit my private sympathies for gentle, stubble-bearded Anthony. Well into his saga years, Anthony, for years Bishops Lydeard's commanding presence, had made way for fresh-faced, bespectacled Henry.

All went serenely before Henry inexplicably heaved and missed toppling forwards out of his crease. Then came a momentary blur of a pirouette and a bat lunge that was simultaneous to behind the wicket ball juggling and a squawked stumping appeal. Was his foot in? Was his bat grounded? Was it in the air? Difficult, difficult. Oh to hell with it, it was down to my middle-age instinct. I raised the finger.

"Generous, Ump, generous," came gully's approval, so ending my umpiring career.

But, of course, there are the consummate professionals. Possibly inspired by a Bill Alley tale, Bill Symonds a very tall, immaculately dressed, former Rhodesian bush pilot always kept a hundred link chain in his deep, spotlessly clean coat pocket when umpiring in the West Somerset league. It was best to be prepared.

For those not in the know the length of a cricket pitch, that's to say the distance between the wickets is measured as a chain, a measure thought up in 1620 by Edmund Gunter, a clergyman, as a low-tech method of accurately surveying land. What became known as 'Gunter's chain' was twenty-two yards long. Simple. How could one go wrong?

Bill Symonds knew there is always a possibility ever since the Leicestershire groundstaff at Ashby-de-la-Zouch had egg on their faces after Somerset arrived for a match. With the Foxes having elected to bat but before the start of play Bill Alley strolled down the pitch from one end to the other and said to umpire Fred Price: "Fred, this wicket's short."

"Don't talk so daft" said Fred.

Bill Alley though was adamant. "I'm telling you, it's not twenty-two yards long."

Fred called for the chain links, put a stump in one end, stretched the link of chain out to its full extent and found that the wicket was a yard short.

Due recognition can be important to the evergreen ego. And it's heady with pride at the honour of being named top umpire in the Somerset League, that postman Richard Disney peddles his cumbersome, parcel-heavy bicycle up Wivey's steep High Street with a certain alacrity that belies his sixty-one years.

Some may quip that Richard is more of an entertainer than a judge but that's only because many venerable locals have long lingering memories in wild, West Somerset. Forty years must now have elapsed since he became legend while on a Wales tour with Huish Champflower. Together with his friend Jesse James, Richard reduced his team-mates into hysterics with an improvised Emu routine by putting his arm up the sleeve of an old coat. Sometimes it's difficult to take such a chap seriously when he sticks up his index digit. More so if that chap was Sammy Woods.

In an anecdote told by the cricket writer Major CHB Pridham tells how Sammy Woods once stood umpire in a first-class match. The Australians were visiting Taunton for their match against Somerset and the Mayor gave them an honorary dinner. Sammy, of course, was a special guest, being not only a great Somerset captain and player of the past, but also an ex-Australian Test cricketer. On rising to respond to a toast he caused much merriment by informing the company that, in consequence of the sudden indisposition of an umpire, he himself would officiate on the morrow, the concluding day of the Somerset v. Australians match. The novel idea of Sammy's umpiring in a first-class match, with his sympathies unevenly divided in favour of the county he had captained so often, evoked general hilarity. When the laughter subsided he added, "But I'll cheat fair!"

Happily, no one would ever have the gall to call Billy Bowden's upraised finger 'crooked'.

Play!

Well, there's one word that moved me when a boy,
That moves today:
It's when the Umpire, to the general joy,
Pronounces 'PLAY!'

May I, ere time with all that he can brin
Of sorrows serried,
Takes that delight from the delight of Spring,
Be dead and buried

By some field path where cricketers may pass
Along its mazes,
And over me the green short English grass,
The English daisies!

Andrew Long.

Then ye contented your souls
With the flannelled fools at the wicket.

The Islanders, Rudyard Kipling.

TWELVE

Leftovers and Constipation

"Leftovers in their less visible form are called memories. Stored in the refrigerator of the mind and the cupboard of the heart."
Thomas Fuller (English Clergyman, 1608-1661).

Although paternalism continues unabated for myself, especially as a kit bag taxi, it's the considered opinion of lauded cricket historians that the condition died within Somerset with the arrival of the mercurial spirited, gossipy WHR Andrews, known simply as 'Bill'. He was a man that believed workers, especially those who worked at the game of cricket, had rights.

"D'you know, he opened his mouth too much but he meant well. And he was often right." This was Cecil Buttle's summing up of Bill, a man who bore a striking resemblance to maybe Nasser Hussein. Or was it Vladimir Putin?

Indeed, John Daniell, the tough as old boots ex-army captain of private means and a forceful, dominating Somerset player, a rock, seldom seen without his Homburg hat and pipe, went so far as to called Bill "a Bolshevik". Perhaps this was because Bill was at heart a humble chap invariably on the side of the ordinary man and who dabbled in local Labour politics. Or maybe it was because Bill made an outrageous demand for higher expenses. Certainly the request was blamed for stuff-shirted Daniell biting through his short pipe. As an amateur he would never have taken a penny of expenses.

Bill's pipe was a long-stemmed pipe, yet it was no pipe of peace that he puffed. To some, he seemed a warrior for justice, to others, a barrack-room lawyer, and given his political leanings, a bowler of 'left' overs. With a perversity later dealt out to the greats of Richards and Garner, Somerset sacked Bill as a player, albeit Bill took the biscuit by suffering the fate twice – in 1932 and 1938. Yet he was the paradigm of Somerset cricket. He arrived via having been a solicitor's teenage clerk and then East Coker professional cum groundsman paid all of three quid a week. The skills he exhibited of white line marking about the wicket he took on a grander scale to the roads as a means of earning winter sustenance.

For Somerset, 750 wickets fell to Bill's late in-swing, including the one of Don Bradman in the year of Bill's second sacking – cruel reward for one who had bowled the 'great man'. Not at all, it was pointed out. Bradman had let himself be bowled quite deliberately after having reached 202, with the second hundred coming in a seventy-minute flurry of finesse. At least the event allowed Bill to adopt his lifelong joke by greeting all a sundry with the greeting "Shake the hand that bowled Bradman".

Opposition batsmen, however, took Bill's bowling seriously. At the Oval, a year before the Bradman affair, he and Arthur Wellard bowled out Surrey for a miserable 35 runs. The match report read: "In six overs and four balls Andrews took eight wickets for 12 runs, and achieved a hat trick". The report didn't mention that Bill had been hobbling, didn't want to bowl on a flat track and left the field rueing that if a boundary catch had been taken his figures would have been stats of true wonderfulness. Instead the offending ball went for 6.

And alongside such bowling achievements one mustn't forget that with his pads on 5,000 runs were garnered courtesy of his bat.

On his 1930 Somerset debut he had asked the Somerset pro Tom Young: "Am I the worst cricketer that ever played first-class cricket, Mr. Young?" "No son," replied Tom, tongue in cheek. "There was one worse than you. Trevor Arnott of Glamorgan." Oh, such subtle high praise, Trevor had dismissed Tom a number of times in the previous two seasons.

With the close of his playing career Bill turned to coaching. Not just at the elite institutions of learning that are Clifton and Millfield, but also at Minehead Middle School where he used his county tie knotted as a belt to keep his trousers up. Yet, such irreverence was nowt compared, it's said, to the libellous and hilarious tales he told as an after-dinner raconteur in the *Rest and Be Thankful*, the pub at Wheddon Cross, a middling tonk away from Exmoor's Dunkery Beacon.

With the distant whistles of West Somerset Railway's smoke-puffing steam trains and the raucous cries of circling seagulls in my ears I sat scorebook on lap, a parental volunteer, for Minehead versus Wiveliscombe Under 15s in a camping chair outside the wooden kit-store hut of that Middle school. I gazed out over a pitch of irregular bounce, made such by the mud-clagged boots and nose-dive divots of winter's rugby. Blimey, I mused, all power to Bill for trying to teach cricket skills here.

Whatever his triumphs might have been over adversity, little seemed to have been handed down to the generation in front of my eyes. Although to be fair several hands-in-pockets youngsters, I noticed, given the restrictions posed by the code of white attire, were dressed somewhat idiosyncratically.

Having inked in singular snicks, dot balls, wides and byes, I then scribbled an apology in the margin for the blot of seagull poo, splattered from on high, smearing across the bowling figures of Stevens, Wood and Staboulis.

"Ah, the annual seagull hit," said my Minehead counterpart, smiling first at my page then at his immaculate one. "Thanks for taking it for me. And for more than likely giving immunity to the record of that other annual treat here, the encounter between the lifeboat bods and the doctors."

I wished the gulls constipation.

As fate would have it, in the not too distant past the Minehead lifeboat fund had worthwhile contributions made to the inflatable prices with the help of a fine constipatory remedy. Well, by the generosity any rate of the drug company that manufactured the medical concoction. No problems of being up one's own arse, Bill might have helpfully said.

The company's involvement came by invitation – a jolly wheeze dreamed up by Bryan, a partner in the town's Harley House surgery who was also then a member of the lifeboat crew. Bryan knew money had been needed to keep the boat in service since 1901 when the lifeboat station was constructed at a cost of £785. In the intervening years wood and oars have made way for motorised inflatables with lifeboat *Bessie* being the latest of the air filled incumbents.

All Bryan did was have a word in the ear of the Duphalac rep. The arrangement was simple. Twenty overs a side. Every player except the wicky to bowl two overs each. The company would donate £1 for each run scored by the medical team and £5 for each lifeboat wicket taken, the accumulated proceeds would be donated to the RNLI. Prescribing practice however couldn't possibly be influenced. Or could it?

First up, Paul, a former RAF medical officer and a GP at Harley House's neighbouring practice, bagged the job of getting to wear the big gloves and pads to keep wicket. "The ball's so bloody hard it hurts if you're skilled or lucky enough to catch it without protection," was his practical reasoning. Mind you, Geoffrey, a retired local surgeon, had the same clever idea, so the two guys played stumper alternate years until Paul graciously acquiesced. Geoffrey had deviously begun to grumble that although still able to stand and lean on his willow he was too old and decrepit to trot after the ball should he have to field.

Paul turned his attention to batting both as therapy for feeling miffed and to put right his performance in the first lifeboat match that he played in and which his wife and four children came in force to watch. Between his medical practice and Harley House only eight doctors could be mustered. The team was a few 'men' short so women were called upon to do their duty and Nina, a partner in Paul's surgery, rose to the occasion. Witnesses to her canny bowling style are known to have remarked there was much reason for remembering the truism that it was a lady not a bloke who developed the first overarm bowling style.

The rest of the doctors' team was made up of offspring able enough to stand and hold a bat. The collective whole, Paul admitted, was absolutely awful. "Look, Daddy's batting, watch Daddy hit the ball and run," he heard his wife say as he faced his first ball and fell for a golden duck. In the following years Paul set himself a target, the fragile property of a Minehead Hospital X-ray department radiographer – Miss Northover's greenhouse. Only once he was successful and it became his crowning glory. "The shattering glass has a strangely evocative effect," he reflected.

Paul performances sort of set the trend for his team around him. The fellow given the partnership job because of his renowned athletic qualities on the rugby field proved a disappointing flop. Supposedly the secret weapon, although prodigiously skilled with a large, oval ball, he was totally inept with a small, round one.

The Duphalac match was high on the calendar of events especially with the Duphalac Man turning up with cratefuls of scrumpy. And of course the lifeboat always did their best to bowl dollies knowing that it was in their best financial interests to do so. Such philanthropy though was on a rather sticky wicket in the decade before the turn of the millennium. The 'powers-that-be' whinged that it wasn't ethical even before the bringing in of drug company rules over sponsorship put a stop to the fundraising element of the game. However, the tradition continued for fun, or as Paul put it, "for the humiliation".

Such a sense of underachievement was also keenly felt by Wivey's Under 15s as, after I had closed the gull-stained scorebook of embarrassments, myself and like-minded brethren of paternal, and indeed maternal mind, taxied homewards with our charges.

Any hope of witnessing even an honourable tie had been too much to hope for. Bill though, but for his death in 1989, would probably have been pleasantly pleased. At least in Minehead, where constipatory runs seemed to be an oxymoron, the town displayed a distinct absence of stuffed shirts.

Tailend Wagging

THIRTEEN

A Return to Dog Days

"If you don't own a dog, at least one, there is not necessarily anything wrong with you, but there may be something wrong with your life."
Roger Caras (American writer and wildlife photographer,1928-2001).

The wicket-keeper was standing back to the slow left-armer. The batsman by all accounts had indulged in a surfeit of scrumpy and potent curry off a pub 'specials' lunch menu before the match.

And the dog days were with us again. The tail was wagging. Those 'dies caniculares', the hottest, most sultry days of summer. An evil time according to Brady's *Clavis Calendarium* of 1813 "when the seas boiled, wine turned sour, Quinto raged in anger, dogs grew mad, and all creatures became languid, causing to man burning fevers, hysterics, and phrensies."

Toby the black and white terrier was having a ball. The ball. And his intention was clear. The younger members of the Brompton Ralph 2nd XI were called upon to use their reservoirs of youthful energy in the task of leashing their problematic twelfth man whose small framed twists and turns made him harder to catch than those infamous test match streakers. *Clavis Calendarium* was certainly right about the "hysterics and phrensies".

"Put the bloody ball in yer pocket until they've got 'im," the square leg umpire ordered in a rare, good decision that afternoon. The demand was really quite sensible, and was met by Brompton Ralph's blood-and-thunder fast bowler gingerly doing with the slobbery cherry what he was told.

With Toby panting but happy and finally tied to the club house handrail, a thought struck me as I sat on the steps of the *Three Ferrets* amongst the more restrained terriers and labradors admiring the exploits of their masters as balls trickled between legs to reach the boundary rope. Although more often than not Lydeard St Lawrence bats swished at the air making no contact with anything other than droplets of sweat. As pets went, cricket, I thought, was a doggy thing. Cats wouldn't be seen dead at a match. Certainly I had never seen one. Felines, and I conjured an image of my own aged puss, tended to restrict their interest to curling up by the radio or on a comfy sofa near Sky reception. It was definitely dogs that had the potential to be the greater problem.

The assertion was soon proven on my return home. "Dear God!" ranted Les from two doors down the street. Someone's best friend had done something beastly in Les's front garden. "I've got a soft spot for mutts like this – a bog in the middle of Exmoor!"

The Wisden Cricketer of the Year 1980, the dog-phobic, master Indian batsman Sunny Gavaskar would have surely echoed Les's sentiments. And had he known that such a place as an Exmoor bog existed during his 1980 season at Somerset then he might have suggested that it be shown to the canine acquaintances that Sir Ian Botham mischievously invited into the Somerset dressing-room.

Indeed, if a dog couldn't be found Sir Ian wasn't shy of making a few hidden woofs of his own. Little surprise Sunny performed better away from Taunton and Sir Ian's tomfoolery. A point proved after opening with Martin Olive at Weston-Super-Mare's St Clarence Park against Yorkshire. With Sir Ian absent from the team, Sunny hit his top score for Somerset, 155 not out. By all accounts there wasn't a dog in sight.

And it's been suggested that Sunny's nickname of 'Swoop' evolved out of his phobia rather than due his feeding a brand of bird seed to the pigeons that amassed on the window sill of his Taunton flat. Those acts kindness followed on from providing succour to what Sunny took to be lonely bird, but one, as it turned out, that had friends. As Peter Roebuck suggests, Swoop was "a loose description of Sunny's fielding at mid-on" because Sunny never dived; a habit borne of dogs making diving in India ruddy dangerous. Toxicariasis and zoonotic6 were ever-present dangers, and feared injections followed close encounters with any foul up.

So knowing the County Ground's history, seeing Sunny there was, to some, a little surprising. Certainly so given that greyhounds had been a popular attraction at the County Ground after the War racing their circles around the outfield, and that as a result woofers in general felt entitled to pad in the pawsteps of their athletic brethren.

Come cricketing match days dogs a plenty, large and small, could be found on the boundary edge taking in the rays for hours on end, filled water bowls at their sides, as their spectator masters peered through binoculars or scanned the back pages of the broadsheets, keeping abreast of cricket scores elsewhere. It wouldn't have been rocket science for Sunny to have guessed from where Sir Ian had courteously 'borrowed'.

Sunny however came too late to Somerset to be introduced to Thumper. At home, sat in his comfy armchair, Mervyn Kitchen, having become a rotund Mendip Acorn and enjoying tours and the cocktails of Malaysia, Singapore and Hong Kong, chuckled with me at the memory of Sir Ian's antics. Then he turned his head to look lovingly at an 'in memoriam' photograph on the shelf behind him of his pet chow.

"That dog was always at the County Ground," he said, "never a problem to anyone until one day at the beginning of the 1970s Roy Virgin and I went out to open the innings.

"Thumper was left on the concrete steps. My wife had gone up town shopping and she'd left the dog with a friend of ours. As I walked out he gate and on to the pitch, I heard a little snigger. I looked over my shoulder and the dog was following about fifteen yard behind. So I turned at Roy and said, 'Bloody dog's following me out.'

"'That's all right,' he said, 'You go up the top end and I'll go down the bottom end.'

"I said, 'OK.'

"So I walked towards the Riverside end of the ground to start the innings, and as I'm approaching the wicket up there, John Langridge, the old Sussex player who was umpiring in them days turned to me and said, 'Mervyn, is that your dog down there?'

"And I said, 'Yes, I'm afraid he's followed us out, John.'

"So he says, 'I think you'd better look round 'cos he's peeing all over the wicket.'

"And I looked round and Thumper actually had his leg cocked over the stumps."

The stumps, however, were generally inaccessible to the general masses. Too late for Sunny, dogs appear absent from the County Ground these days. This might have something to do with the passing of the ground's poplar trees to make way for the concrete of high rising retirement flats and new stands. Gone with the trees are the pooches amenities of convenience.

Knowing what dogs are capable of it's unsurprising that some clubs, even local ones, take 'measures'. Succinct to the point of detriment, "No dogs" is the sign beheld by visitors to Dulverton Cricket Club. Unfortunately, it's not a very big sign and can easily be overlooked by the distracted, or indeed those turning a blind eye. However, to ignore it can cause a degree of umbrage to home parties. Yet, it was not for me to cast aspersions as to the cause of Lexi, a black Labrador, not long out of puppydom and belonging to Wivey's captain Dennis being taken for a pre-match 'bounce' on the outfield by Dennis's wife.

She claimed innocence. Dulverton claimed a wind-up. And Adrian, Dulverton's skipper, shouted a bit rudely about degrees of literacy. So just let it be said that things had rather got off on the wrong paw before Lexi was confined to the car boot. Dennis frowned.

Then his frown got worse. Batting first, Wivey were all out for a miserable 43 in what was to prove to be the day of the educator.

Burnham schoolteacher and opener Paul had top scored with twenty odd. And but for his presence and some over-excited waywardness by the Dulverton bowling attack, it might well have been a case of the 8 of 1857 revisited as, at the other end, Paul witnessed a procession. Partners came and went with alarming rapidity. Extras second top scored. The third top score was 4.

Of course there were grumbles about the pitch. "'Tis the opposite to a shirt-front," "A tad green," and "An absolute 'road' only suitable for Flintstones' cricket," were merely expressions of Wivey opinion on the cusp of the tea interval.

Life though has its counterbalances that lessen the pain of indignity. Yes, Dulverton's men had seemingly excelled themselves but so had their women-folk. Created in the line of duty, 'tea' was a fortifying spread of local pride and magnificence laid out in a clubhouse that could itself only be described as lavish: Victoria sponges and chocolate cakes warm from the Rayburns and Agas of the Exmoor town, sausage rolls in the finest of flaky puff pastry, triangles of chilled salmon and cucumber sandwiches and scrummy scones generously topped with strawberry jam and thick clotted cream. Indeed, as clubhouse blowouts go Dulverton's are considered by cricketing tea-time connoisseurs to be the very best in the West Somerset League.

However, if such foodie heaven was a cunning home team ploy, against Wivey that day it failed. On the resumption of play, as all about held distended tummies and moved sloth-like in torpor, enter 'The Master'. Or to be exact Jimmy Beale, Headmaster of Taunton Preparatory School, Wivey's right-arm spearhead pacer and, most importantly, a man of sterling constitution. It was a light he had kept under a bushel. To the amazement of teammates he got a 'five fer' haul. Or was it a 'six fer'? Nobody of Wivey, least of all Jimmy, really cared. With balls kept in the 'corridor' they thudded into pads, stern "howzats?" encouraged umpires into digit-raising, and stumps were disarrayed. As Jimmy had demolished tea so he demolished Dulverton. They were routed for 39.

However, it wasn't as if Dulverton had suffered from complacency. "Dog of a pitch, that," observed Dennis in an off-the-cuff post match analysis to nobody in particular.

Stood within earshot, a middle-aged woman was suddenly spurred to high dudgeon. "How dare you. My Dad spends every hour God gives preparing that pitch," she sniped, just at the moment Dennis's wife decided to give Lexi another airing to enjoy the scent of victory and the contents of a saved 'doggy-bag'.

It was all too much for Adrian. Obviously upset by the afternoon's turn of events, he went into a loud apoplectic rant aimed not at Lexi but at Lexi's mistress.

"Don't shout at my wife like that," riposted Dennis tapping Adrian on the shoulder.

Understandably, tension was pretty high when the labrador finally left the ground, escorted away by an entourage that included a Wivey team which to a man was drunk on success and the befuddlement of disbelief that the game had been won. Behind stayed the good women of Dulverton cleaning up what few crumbs remained from their lovingly prepared repast of home baking.

Around the *Three Ferrets*, with the abundance of 'laissez faire', of hedges and bark-coated trunks, there is a sense of far less stress and anxiety on dog day afternoons.

Gavaskar Calypso

It was Gavaskar
The real master
Just like a wall
We couldn't out Gavaskar at all
Not at all
You know the West Indies couldn't out Gavaskar at all.

Lord Relator

FOURTEEN

Of Hippies, Hollywood and Crown Jewels

*"No rules exist, and examples are simply life-savers answering
the appeals of rules making vain attempts to exist."*

Andre Breton (French Poet and co-Founder of surrealism, 1896-1966).

Although nomadic teams are born out of any number of necessities, like not bothering with home pitch, rarely does a club, apart from in name only, not actually exist at all. This might seem like gobbledegook, but rest assured, for one team I chanced upon this is the case. And they only play one match a year.

I had only been half listening to the table banter of Mooseman and Phil as I bibbled in the 'Bearin' Up', staring as I was into my half full pint glass of cider, reliving my life's only hat-trick. A memory drawn from the halcyon days of being a long-haired, bum-fluff-chinned student of lazy ambition playing in a match against the eclectic staff of East Devon College upon Stoodleigh's Elysian field set amongst rhododendrons in the Exe Valley. There was me ever hoping for spin from my slow right-arm pies. Mills of Psychology bowled between bat and pad by a lucky straight one. Hoffman of History stumped after falling over while yahooing at one gently passing by his backside. And Smith of Engineering, having middled it, caught at cow corner by Commie Lenny, the college hippie. "Like plucking a cherry from a tree," said Lenny.

He was too modest. My joy was unconfined, my incredulity enormous. Not least because Lenny's catch had been the most amazing of feats given that a short while earlier he had been lying prostrate on his back on the boundary edge allowing a steady trickle from the tap of the scrumpy barrel, sat on the trestle table above him, to flow into his lusting maw.

My sigh of nostalgic contentment was curtailed as I was abruptly brought out of my reverie and back into the land of the living. "What cricket game in pyjamas?" I asked, with a sudden blink of interest.

"Not pyjamas, Chazzer. 'PJ'. I was talking about PJ's game," chided Moose-man, gently. "PJ Brice, an Englishman from Hollywood, is flying in from the States to play at Brompton Ralph at the weekend with Manhattan Cricket Club. They do it every year, the first Sunday in August, regular as clockwork. PJ's a local lad made good apparently – a wealthy young soul whose team's made up of a load of his old mates. They're up against some lot led by a tax lawyer. Bet you didn't know PJ's played for the Hollywood and Beverley Hills Cricket Club and played in the Ashes. That's 'Stars-ville' that is."

"Golly, how exciting!" I exclaimed, reckoning that my own bush telegraph had let me down badly. Was PJ some erstwhile Gary Pratt of Oval fame running out the likes of Punter Ponting?

"Manhattan's got history," I said, sticking to the known facts. New York cricket dated back to 1751, when team 'New York' bowled in Manhattan against a 'London XI' in the first recorded American match. And to top that, in 1844, the world's first international match also took place in Manhattan when Canada and the United States competed at St George's Cricket Club. Interestingly, they did so under new rules.

Up until 1830 charging had been permitted. This was nothing to do with selling tickets. Rather that batsmen, either already out or those waiting to bat, could charge fielders in the American football fashion to hinder them stop-ping any ball thumped towards the boundary. No doubt it would have been an immensely entertaining, though chaotic, spectacle to witness. Now an esti-mated twenty percent of New York City's eight million residents emigrated from a country where cricket was the main sport. Most notably perhaps is the former Glastonbury player, Guyana-born Steve Massiah.

Yet, whereas the likes of James Hildreth and Wes Durston turned out for Glas-tonbury before becoming county professionals, Steve not only turned down a contact from Nottinghamshire but also turned his back on England alto-gether, preferring instead to head States side. By all accounts he currently plays in the Nassau League, the worst league in New York that's not even, it's said, suited to schoolboys. The positive for Steve, however, is that he's captain of the US team, a team that he's been a part of for a decade.

Unfortunately, Glastonbury Cricket Club playing as it does in the West of England premier league, the top level for amateur cricket, had now got itself into the news for all the wrong reasons. A sightscreen had been demolished, nets torn and wicket covers defaced. £4000 of damage in all. Vandals were blamed – "a bunch of bird-brained nincompoops", Mooseman called them.

I just hoped the rozzers caught up with such bad apples instead of setting surprise mercury gun speed traps for those keen not to miss a toss. For my part, I needed to catch up with PJ Who exactly was he? My head was abuzz. Perhaps he was a newer version of Lord Tim Hudson the ex-public schoolboy turned wealthy erotic artist, via property developing and the voice of characters in the Disney cartoons *The Jungle Book* and *The Aristocats,* who moved to England and bought one of the most beautiful cricket grounds in all of England, the Birtles Bowl. Now, as I keypad tap this, the pitch is overgrown and up for sale.

Back in the 1980s the *London Times* roared that Lord Tim wanted to build "Rock and Roll Cricket". What he created was Hudson's Hollywood XI and staged the event of the decade, a ten thousand pounds, winner-takes-all cricket match between the greats of the game. Macclesfield was where Test match met 'flower power', with Lord Tim describing cricket as "the best trip I ever had".

And they were Cheshire times that had those wild knights of 'blood brothers' Sir Viv Richards and Sir Ian Botham strutting their stuff in stripe bright blazers of green, black, yellow and red. Panama hats, margarita cocktails and Krug in the psychedelically painted 'rainbow' pavilion were de rigueur in those crazed days. Days which saw Beefy spread-eagled in the back of a vintage motor, smoking a cigar as he was driven to the ground.

As it turned out PJ was no ex-public schoolboy, not a bit of it. And neither was he a hippie. Nor a Gary Pratt.

This I discovered after I had pitched up late outside the *Three Ferrets* on match day. The game was well underway, a guy in a pair of very dark sunglasses caught my arm to tell me about Sammy Woods hiding cider bottles in hedgerows, and a petite lady in jean shorts, was selling raffle tickets. Cadged into buying a strip to aid a donation to Taunton's Musgrove Park Hospital Breast Care Ward, I discovered the lady to be PJ's mother Susan. Welcomed, she introduced me to Mr Blacker – the man of the shades – and assured me that it was his real name. I asked her about the day's goings on.

Well, it was thirty overs a side. Most important, the team in the field wasn't the Manhattan Cricket Club but the Manhattan *Beach* Cricket Club. To prove the point a sweaty young man arrived at the boundary red-faced and puffing after a forlorn ball chase. His T-shirt sported a rather fetching blue logo depicting an American lifeguard station. I recognised its likeness from *Baywatch*. Susan was thrilled that the logo was conceived by a girl in the design studio of PJ's own LA-based marketing business.

"Way to go, Silver Fox! Great batting!" came a shout from the sprawl of players, dogs broken bats, prams and babies toys gathered around the scoreboard and portacabin clubhouse a few metres from where Susan and I stood.

"The opposition's in good voice," I remarked. "They seem an eclectic mix." Playing shirts bore club badges from across Somerset – Temple Cloud, Wellington, Stogumber and Bridgwater, to name just a few. "Who's the Silver Fox?"

"Oh, that's Jim Greenhough. He's Milverton's Chairman."

"Is he the tax lawyer?"

"No. That's Stuart Thorne, the one in the splendid red cap. It's his eleven. He scored a hundred yesterday for Staplegrove," said Susan pointing towards a burly man in jovial spirits, his face creased by laughter lines, padding up."

"Ah, not quite what I expected," I said before my eye was caught by a bright glint from the middle.

Its blade bright with a sparkly maker's decal, the bling bat of the Silver Fox had suddenly flashed and sun dazzled before Pitsford Hill reverberated to the sound of a loud bovine bellow of protest as ball hit rump. In a blink of a watery eye Cow Corner became Bullock Bottom and the fence-rubbing herd dispersed, seeking safety from further boundary bombardment of such massive nature.

I felt prompted to ask whether Jim was called the Silver Fox because of his hair or his bat but refrained, asking instead for Susan to point out PJ. I followed the line of her finger to mid on where there stood a thirty-something six-footer of Freddie Flintoff build and Freddie Flintoff designer fuzz, looking a little jet lagged. Unless my eyes deceived me this was definitely not a Tim Hudson.

"A long way to come for a game of cricket," I said matter-of-factly. "Why?"

Susan sighed. "You really need to talk to Michael, my husband. He'll tell you everything you want to know. He got a mention in Ian Botham's autobiography. Isn't that wonderful? He's somewhere in the clubhouse."

Michael turned out to be an affable, tall, thin chap of middling years, and the whole Manhattan Beach Cricket Club affair had been the brainchild of him and Susan – an opportunity for PJ to return home from the States for a sociable game of cricket offering the chance to reunite with friends from school and university, and for Michael and Susan to meet up with friends from their own college days. A way of keeping the ties, so to speak. One couple had come from as far afield as Reading. Stuart the Lawyer he had known since they were in childhood – a time when Milverton had chanced to take on the Uganda Kobs, some Bohemians and even the Gas Board.

Susan sidled up to gloss things over further. While studying at Somerset College of Arts and Technology in the early '70s she and her bunch of girlfriends met a bunch of young chaps who at the time were all police cadets. They paired up and each pair ended up marrying one another. It was funny she thought how none of the men ended up remaining in the police. Each opted for a less uniform means of existence. And this was the 'club's' seventh match in seven years – the most important event in the family calendar. The previous year the wedding of PJ's sister Emma was arranged around it.

At this point Michael gave a politic cough.

After enlightening me that Susan was appointed, after "due discussion", as Chairperson and as 'officer-in-chief' of all organisation, and that it was her job to select the Manhattan Beach team, Michael began bantering with a fellow of similar vintage who retained the arch-backed stance of a purist batsman of the Peter Roebuck ilk.

Over past years Michael had regularly opened for Milverton with Adrian Keates, the arch-backed fellow. By all accounts they had been an enduring pair known as 'Smash' and 'Grab', with Adrian taking on the role of Smash with a habit of shattering the glass of greenhouses from a distance.

I asked Michael for some cricketing memories. His reply didn't quite meet the game's romantic image. "I vividly remember Knowle," he said, "a fairly rough area of Bristol with an urban pitch surrounded by a boundary edge graffitied brick wall. A bloke walking his muzzled rottweiler shouted 'Nice throw, Rachael!' at me. I decided not to object too much. Still, playing there must toughen you up. Australia's Mike Beer played for them."

As I scribbled that last little titbit of information into my black Moleskine Michael continued to reminisce.

"Then there was Parnells at Paulton, just after the Chernobyl disaster when hill sheep went radioactive in Wales. I spent the whole match staring nervously skywards and it wasn't for descending balls. Mind you, the only balls I had real cause to worry about were my own. As a lad in the Somerset indoor nets, a ball hit me in the 'crown jewels'. Pole-axed me. Through my watering eyes Bill Andrews appeared to approach with what looked like a groping hand, offering me his assistance. Of course, I groaned that I was 'fine'."

"Was this why he was called Grab?" I enquired. As he explained it was more to do with nurdling and caressing quick singles, the sound of whoops and polite clapping came from the outside world. Michael Eele, whose brother was umpiring in straw hat and shorts, had taken a regulation catch at Bullock Bottom. The Silver Fox was gone. Stuart the Lawyer was in.

Quack. By 'Sod's Law' Stuart was out for a golden duck, snicking his first ball into the wicketkeeper's gloves. The calamity momentarily caused him to lose his sense of humour. Composure regained on the trudge back, and having joined Michael, he waxed lyrically to me about mishaps befalling a more illustrious captain, the West Indies Richie Richardson. Stuart, it tran-spired, had been Richie's skipper during a spell at Staplegrove.

Batting with John Jameson, ex-Taunton School and Warwickshire, Richie was hit in 'the lunchbox'. In similar fashion to Michael's misadventure, he too was pole-axed. Stuart suggested to Richie that he be "nipped off to hospital" where his bollocks would be "off in a minute". "No man, I'm okay, I'm okay. I'll keep on batting," Richie gasped. He went on to hit 73.

Come Staplegrove's turn to field Richie ran to retrieve the ball from a dense patch of stinging nettles. "Oh, there're snakes, man! There're snakes!" yelped the beleaguered West Indian doing an impression of Fred Astaire with St Vitus' dance, or, indeed, of Hallam Moseley, the kind, gentle Somerset No. 11 with jumbled-arm bowling action. One of the Somerset legends, he had been recommended by none other than Sir Garfield Sobers. His benefit game organised by Timsbury Cricket Club when Somerset were at the peak of their Golden Era proved to be particularly lucrative. Aside from Hallam signing autographs the match was highlighted by Sir Ian Botham keeping wicket and delighting a large 'well-oiled' crowd with a typically swashbuckling century that included eight sixes and ten fours on a picturesque village green beside which Dennis Breakwell, from reliable accounts, hid behind a tree.

Now long retired but still doing a bit of coaching at Lord's, Hallam went by the nickname of 'Seymour' due to him having resembled the noble West Indian batsman Seymour Nurse, rather than because of thick spectacles held in place by an elastic band affair. However, even with the world in focus, Hallam once famously couldn't find the ball for the nettles. And as with Richie, if any kind soul thought to warn the Barbadian as to the hazards of

English flora, he held his peace.

And when it came to mentioning talented West Indians in the 'Shrubbery', there was a consensus that Watchet's Guyanese-born Andy Iffel was also one of the best. A comment from a chap in a Wellington shirt of "Blimey he was quick," met with agreeing nods. Andy's bowling figures of 8-29 against Wellington in 1995 remain almost unrivalled in the Division 1 of the Somerset League.

I asked Michael who the fastest bowler was he had ever faced. Without hesitation he replied, "Nigel Popplewell". Stuart smiled, and well he might. After retiring from first- class cricket Nigel had exchanged his grubby raincoat that he used to train in, and which his team-mates were unable to bin seasons on end, for a pin-striped suit and joined Stuart's solicitors' practice.

Leaving Michael and Stuart reminiscing I eventually caught up with PJ down to bat at 7 for Manhattan Beach. It came as a revelation that he was a product of Wivey's Kingsmead Community School, not a hundred yards from my warped blue front door. Indeed, he had made good.

Describing himself as "a Los Angeles businessman who cossets a romanticism of home", PJ told me that he was very proud to be an Englishman in America. And it was something that he refused to dilute. He ensured business meetings were reserved for Mayfair rather than in any of our predominantly metal-shuttered, seedy urban wastelands. In Blighty this time for just two days, rural life for him still revolved around cricket and the *Three Ferrets*, where Brompton Ralph's sweated changing rooms benefit aeration by sweet Somerset breeze.

And PJ did play for the Hollywood and Beverly Hills Cricket Club. However, there was still that question about the Ashes.

It transpired that Mooseman hadn't got the full picture. However, the reality was no less remarkable, particularly for a young man raised in the Somerset sticks. Having become well connected PJ's cricketing efforts had led him to bat valiantly with England captain Graeme Hick to try and save the day against Australia in the *Hollywood* Ashes.

The event was conceived by a group of cricket enthusiasts in the Hollywood Hills watching a satellite feed of the 2006/7 Ashes series and it was decided that LA needed its own legendary tussle between cricket's oldest foes. The Honorary Board boasted Sir John Major, Sir Michael Parkinson, Rupert Murdoch, Ozzy Osbourne, Hugh Jackman, Kevin Pietersen, and Shane Warne. What took place was a Twenty20 match. Australia were led by

Michael Kasprowicz, the former right-arm fast test match bowler.

Tracey Ullman tossed the coin. Graeme Hick won toss and decided to field.

Reports noted about 1,750 picnicking spectators "filling themselves full with Longshot coffee, Red Bull and Four 'n' Twenty pies". Reports also noted that the Australian Consulate General had decreed: "Under no circumstances should the Aussie team lose the match". They didn't – hitting 153 for 9, they won by 19 runs thanks largely to actor Cameron Daddo scoring 23 runs from just 17 balls. Prior to this exhibition of explosive shot play Cameron's tour de force had been as Professor Lovecraft in *Pterodactyl*, a woefully bad monster movie in which explorers fight for survival after accidentally awakening a clutch of long-dormant dinosaurs deep within a volcano in the middle of the Turkish jungle.

At close of play at Brompton Ralph the scorecard read: The Stuart Thorne XI: 295 for 7 off 30 overs, Manhattan Beach CC: 261 for 8 off 30 overs. PJ Brice's bowling figures were 0 for 22, and batted at number 8, he scored 10 before being caught. It was a long way to come by plane and train to concede more than double than what he managed with the bat. But that wasn't what the day was really about.

As I headed home to my warped blue front door my thoughts were of an extraordinary cricket match, of an August afternoon that had proved to be most illuminating, and of Roy, the heart and soul of Brompton Ralph cricket who first battled the Pitsford Hill buttercups, winning the raffle. And to that end the Manhattan Beach Cricket Club logo, I decided, was absolutely appropriate. The money raised amongst friends was indeed lifesaving.

FIFTEEN

Strange Figures

"I see figures, strange figures, weird figures."
Groucho Marx, Animal Crackers (1930).

My turning to the sports pages of the morning's *Daily Telegraph* bought when September was infant and early mist hung in Taunton Vale caused me to wipe my reading glasses. And although not having the cleanest of tissues in my pocket I felt the need to wipe them again before squinting at the back page. Really it was most odd, I thought. Brian Anthony Langford's bowling figures had got a mention. He had retired decades ago. Then again he had quite often found himself involved in a newsworthy story.

For instance there was the one Mervyn Kitchen tells of Charles Carter, the army officer's son who always kept wicket wearing a cravat. He was keen as keen can be but had never had many victims stumped. On Bath's turning wicket in 1969, during a County Championship match that Somerset staggeringly won by two runs, Hampshire's famous South African batsman Barry Richards charged a spinning off-break halfway down the wicket. The ball went through the gate and into Charles's gloves. Instead of doing the usual thing of just knocking off a bail, with great arm leverage Charles took a mighty side-swipe and knocked all three stumps flat out of the ground before appealing for a stumping. "Not out," said the umpire Oswald Herman, a former Hampshire man himself. The Somerset bowler had been Brian.

Now, behind the Somerset stand at the County Ground, Brian has become a man honoured by having a blown up sepia photograph of himself tacked to the nicely pointed wall in the alley through which the wind whistles scurrying leaves, and where cheers and groans echo. This is Somerset's Hall of Fame, and here, just to the right of the door to the men's loos, is Brian's team-mate 'Dasher' Denning lovingly remembered for his country yokel image of unruly blond hair, white floppy hat and adoration of the Wurzels. Perhaps his image was whimsically placed in just that particular spot to amuse some Committee wit.

Tragically dying from cancer aged only 57 in the summer of 2007 Dasher, the Chewton Mendip butcher's son who invented the Chewton chop, had been a specialist one day mumbling wonder in the 1970s.

Healthier than the Barnsley chop, unless an unfortunate happened to be dozing in the field anywhere from cover point to slip, Dasher's chop was an ingenious cut of a cricket ball rather than a greedy cut of lamb. Choosing cricket over school-mastering, he was a rarity of a sportsman, being disin-clined to boast. Once, having removed his seemingly over-sized pads after another innings of propelling balls niftily into boundary boards, he was asked to do a BBC radio interview:

"Well, now, after this great, great performance today, you'll be looking forward to greater things."

(Indistinguishable mumble.)

"D'you expect to be in the England side soon?"

"Er, no."

"But why do you say that?"

"Not good enough."

As a man of character Dasher could only have played for Somerset. Brian Rose remarked: "He was hard, stubborn and made it difficult for the oppo-sition – especially when he growled at them!" He may never have worn the badge of the three lions, but he always battled his best for the dragon beast that flew from the pavilion flagstaff. It meant everything, as it did to Brian Langford.

Just over forty years ago on a warm July Sunday afternoon Langford skip-pered a team that included Dasher, as well the Aussie Greg Chappell and some others now elevated to 'The Wall', namely 'Rosey', Roy Virgin, Merv Kitchen and 'Budgie' Burgess.

Somerset were playing Essex in a John Player League match at Yeovil's Johnson Park, named after Stanley Johnson, a glove manufacturer who had donated the field at the end of the Second World War.

Brian won the toss and decided to field. After scoring a paltry single with the bat, he recorded bizarre one day figures with his off-spin. In a low scoring match that the home team won by a couple of wickets chasing down 120 odd, his figures read: eight overs, eight maidens, no runs, no wickets – making today's frugal bowling of Alfonso Thomas resemble profligate money lending in the credit crunch.

As a reward Brian had his photograph taken. Come early September 2010 he had it taken again while Somerset, led by 'Trigger' Trego, took on to the Pakistani tourists – a truly sombre affair in which no spectator got drunk or got thrown out of the ground, and the world was in the throes of 'Noball-gate' of match fixing. Brian had smiled into the lens with his arm around the shoulder of the seventy-five year old Pakistani team manager Yawar Saeed.

Somerset lost the game by eight runs. The two teams had first met at Taunton in 1954 and Yawar had played in that game. Bizarrely, he wore a Somerset cap. Indeed, between 1953 and 1955 he played 50 games for the county. To be frank, the team was pretty poor to say the least. It finished bottom in three of those seasons, but no one seemed to mind too much – even when Yawar, an enthusiastic medium pacer, might have inadvertently overstepped the bowling crease.

Those playing days of his were in a more innocent age. Life then was surely simpler lining up as he did alongside Maurice Tremlett and the West Indian Peter Wight. The latter, a fine number 3 or 4 bat in his pomp, became, at the age of eighty, the oldest living Somerset player to be honoured with his image hung to face the elements in the 'Hall of Fame'.

It was the morning after the latest Pakistan game that I could be forgiven for checking the date in the top left hand corner of the paper. There in black and white were Brian and his Yeovil bowling figures albeit slightly distorted, no doubt by the discrepancies that can creep in over time. He had been awarded a wicket.

Yet there Brian was, mentioned along with Railways (Pakistan) and Dera Ismail Khan, two teams of whom the former had won a match by an innings and 851 runs, and Essex's Norbert Phillip who had taken six for four as Surrey were bowled out for a paltry 14 runs. And there, too, was Sir Ian Terence Botham and his 1981 Ashes batting heroics at Headingley. The penny then dropped, the blooming article, written by cricket correspondent Simon

Hughes, Middlesex's former right-arm fast-medium pacer turned journo and broadcaster, was about the vagaries and possibilities of match-fixing.

Professional cricketers are part athletes, part exhibitionists – players in two senses of the word. The great draw of the game is that it's a cross between sport and theatre.

There is even a Hollywood and Beverley Hills Cricket Club, a social rather than a competitive enterprise that was founded by Errol Flynn and David Niven in 1940s for a 40,000 strong expat community. Beefy had made to prove the point that cricket's actors are masters of putting on a fine show by trying to get into Hollywood after the famous Headingly test that had seen England attain odds of 500-1 to beat Australia. A match which both Rod Marsh and Dennis Lillee put a wager on via their bus driver. And there indeed lay the rub.

The events surrounding "Noballgate' had now persuaded those in the world of cricket to examine every vaguely odd game in a different light. Did Brian Langford's figures at Yeovil in 1969 require scrutiny? Were the Essex batsmen offered free cider in Brian Langford's pub? One can only give a categorical no. Although, to be fair, over the years Somerset have been involved in more than their fair share of oddities, enough to give one heart failure or the heebie-jeebies.

Yet Simon Hughes was posing pertinent questions. Did the Aussies let Beefy get 149 not out? Did they deliberately sacrifice their wickets at Edgbaston as he took five for 11 to steal an English victory by 29 runs? Was Botham actually employed by central casting? Such scurrilous debate was obviously done tongue-in-cheek, otherwise if Nietzsche had discovered cricket he might not have been so very pessimistic.

What else was happening in the world? I asked this question to myself. A perusal of the newpaper's entertainment ads showed bow-tied Henry 'Blowers' Blofeld, that raconteur with the humorous touch of wickedness and mocker of pomposity and pretentiousness, would be coming to the Taunton's Brewhouse Theatre with his new show 'Caught Short And Grumpy'. Peter Denning might well have approved of that.

SOMERSET v ESSEX

Player's County League 1969
Venue: Johnson Park, Yeovil on 27 July 1969 (40-over match)
Somerset won the toss and decided to field
Umpires: J Arnold and JG Langridge

Essex innings

B Ward	hit wicket	b R Palmer	23
*+B Taylor	c Kitchen	b Burgess	8
HR Sherman		b Robinson	2
BL Irvine		c & b Robinson	3
KD Boyce	lbw	b Chappell	46
DJ Insole		run out	0
S Turner		run out	23
BEA Edmeades	lbw	b Chappell	10
RNS Hobbs		b Chappell	8
RE East		run out	2
JK Lever		not out	0
Extras (lb 1)			1
Total (all out, 38.2 overs)			126

Fall of wickets: 1-10, 2-15, 3-19, 4-69, 5-83, 6-85, 7-109, 8-124, 9-126, 10-126.

Somerset bowling: R Palmer: 8-0-37-1, Burgess: 7-2-27-1, Robinson: 8-2-27-2, Langford: 8-8-0-0, Chappell: 7.2-0-34-3.

Somerset innings

+RT Virgin		c & b Boyce	2
A Clarkson	c East	b Boyce	5
GS Chappell		b Edmeades	36
MJ Kitchen	c Boyce	b East	14
PW Denning	c East	b Edmeades	5
BC Rose	lbw	b Edmeades	0
GI Burgess		not out	26
R Palmer		run out	0
*BA Langford		b Boyce	1
PJ Robinson		not out	24
Extras (b 7, lb 7)			14
Total (8 wickets, 39.1 overs)			127

Did not bat: KE Palmer.

Fall of wickets:: 1-6, 2-11, 3-51, 4-63, 5-63, 6-72, 7-73, 8-82.

Essex bowling: Boyce: 8 -4-15-3, Lever: 8-1-28-0, East: 8-2-26-1, Edmeades: 8-4-22-3, Turner: 7.1-1-22-0.

Somerset won by 2 wickets.

SIXTEEN

Impressing the Ladies

"All truths are easy to understand once they are discovered;
the point is to discover them."

Galileo Galilei (Italian Philosopher, Astronomer and
Mathematician, 1564-1642).

That morning, with Taunton now the home of England Women's Cricket, England's women's cricket team were in the town's Starbucks, Somerset's Anya Shrubsole included, where they bore witness to Nick, a goatee-bearded barista, going down on one knee and proposing to his girl-friend Laura. England's ladies whooped "Hooray!" and applauded as she said "yes".

In the old times when England's gentler sex wore knee length, pleated, white skirts they had played at Mitcham Green, used for cricket since 1685 and believed to be the oldest cricket ground in the world. England played Australia here in front of a crowd of 10,000 spectators and more prams, dogs, ice cream men, and bikes than ever seen before anywhere. Trams, buses, cars crashed by on three sides of the ground. And here Wessex schoolmistress Betty Snowball carried the hopes of England as Aussie Mollie Flaherty "thrilled the watching thousands by bowling so hard and fast that one stocking descended, and she then rolled both down and they became ankle socks". That was in 1937.

The point is that ladies have been giving their all to cricket since beyond living memory, ever since the Duke of Dorset during the reign of George III first contemplated, "What is human life but a game of cricket? And if so, why should not the ladies play it as well as we? The ladies know how to handle the ball and bat with the best of us."

Nowadays even little Brompton Ralph up the road had a couple of women's teams. Ladies hereabouts get involved even when not playing the field. And I don't mean just by making the teas. For instance, a lady of boundless energy called Libby Trott was nominated for the 'AgustaWestland Volunteer of the Year Award' by South Somerset District Council for giving her spare time to be the general factotum of small, rural West and Middle Chinnock Cricket Club. Even my cricket quizzical wife had been encouraged to learn the rudimentary rules of the game after catching a mere glimpse of a televised Marcus Trescothick whacking a white ball. Thereafter she was happy to watch cricket from the sofa and opine: "You can see so much more from here." And most encouragingly, her Japanese friend Suki had taken on board that what she had thought were random points were actually called 'runs', the 'wicket' was three upright sticks, with two sticks across on top, and she had been to a T20 game at the County Ground.

So it could never be too late for my next-door neighbour Gill to be cured of her total disinterest in the game. As far as it was believed, Gill's desire to watch cricket, either televised of in actuality, was lower in her life agenda than drowning allotment slugs in stale beer, climbing ladders to dissuade starlings from nesting in her roof, or going to an excessively loud shoegazing rock concert. And in her professional capacity as a proof-reader, something which meant income, she remained extremely non-committal about a publisher's offer for her to cast a practiced eye over a new book on the summer game.

What was needed to entice her towards cricket was a non-negotiable opportunity.

Come early evening that opportunity presented itself. As he bibbled in the 'Bearin' Up' Mooseman was cogitating a return to the County Ground. It would be a catharsis. Not long before he had volunteered along with some others to be a cricket commentator for the blind at the County Ground with the idea being that blind people, or the partially sighted, would be given handsets when they entered the ground and could therefore listen to pertinent wittering.

To discover if Mooseman was potentially any good he was invited to a rehearsal to "paint a picture in words" over soundless video highlights of 'Botham's Ashes', a recording that still gave tingles of delight. The rehearsal was crazy. Highlights have difficulties. Just as he was sorting out field settings, next second someone was bowling and was hit, next second another person was bowling and was hit and he shouted, "Woah!" Gallingly, as he floundered trying to recall the names of the main protagonists, one bloke remembered the name of the blooming umpire as well as every 'baggy green' capped Aussie.

The experience had quite put Mooseman off watching cricket at all. However, he thought the time was ripe to give it another go – purely as a spectator, of course.

And so the decision was made that Mooseman should strike while the iron was hot. The next match was a home T20 against Glamorgan, six years since I had my first blooding of twenty overs a side cricket. In a match that Somerset won by a nail-biting margin of 4 runs they had taken on a Northants team that included Ben Phillips while Somerset had given T20 debuts to Marcus Trescothick and Punter Ponting. How time flies.

"For moral support you could go with Big Jeremy," I suggested to Mooseman. "It's on his birthday. It can be his treat in addition to a fridge full of bittersweet Dabinet cider." Big Jeremy was a gentle giant of an opera singer who would la-la-la his baritone scales each morning through his open bedroom window when he wasn't up in Covent Garden. He also happened to be Gill's hubby.

"What a good idea," said Mooseman. "And Gill would have to come, too. Just think, she might discover a whole new world of excitement."

This indeed was a sound statement. Somerset were excelling themselves in T20 and expectations were high ever since Graeme Smith led the County to cup victory in 2005 and Justin Langer led them to Indian subcontinent success over Deccan Chargers in 2009.

With the Glamorgan match so imminent pub banter turned towards dragons. At the time when ladies suffered from the embarrassment of falling down tights Somerset used to play Glamorgan at Weston-super-Mare to accommodate the hordes of steamy travellers. Many a Welshman justly felt he had a stake in the Campbell paddle steamers of The White Funnel Line and Somerset used to be confident that the morning Campbell would bring over an enthusiastic crowd from Cardiff. Now the Welsh just pelted over the new Severn Bridge and down the M5, readying to mingle their dragon banners with those of the Somerlanders as the two teams did beastly battle at a sun-browned Taunton with an outfield like glass.

"The Somerset flag should be a blackbird," said Mooseman, who then declared matter-of-factly. "We don't sing *Puff the Magic Dragon*, just because there's a dragon flapping on the county pole, do we? We sing 'Where be that blackbird to?' Don't we?"

"Ah," I said wistfully, "colley or raven, jackdaw or crow?
'He sees that this great roundabout
The world, with all its motley rout,
Church, army, physic, law,
Its customs and its businesses,
Is no concern at all of his,
And says — what says he? — Caw.'
The Jackdaw, William Cowper."

"Chazzer's being too clever for his own good," said Fisher John, smirking at me.

John had earned his prefix from his frequent leg-side wafts at the crease rather than for his love of tope fishing, or "topiary" as he called it, in Porlock Bay. "S'pose on the basis of having a blackbird we could just as easily have a yellow Teletubby. Somerset La-La and all that."

"For God's sake, F.J.. It's Somerset-La-la-LA," said Mooseman with a degree of frustration. "Haven't *you* ever been to a home game?"

"Nope."

Mooseman let out a gasp of disbelief. "Oh my! Goodness gracious me! Well, you're coming, too. No argument."

And so the evening of the match arrived. Jeremy took along a celebratory birthday cider-crammed icebox and Gill took a good book, and they ensconced themselves with the gatherings of banners, fancy dressed super-heroes and fluffy Friesian cows. Somerset won by six wickets with Kieron Pollard thumping 19 runs in eleven minutes off 8 balls including three sixes.

Next morning Gill was being her usual Jack-of-all-trades. Or more precisely she was being a 'steeple-Gill' teetering up a ladder tenaciously jamming on a missing end to her plastic guttering that had been dislocated while evicting the attic starlings.

"How was it last night?" I called up the ladder.

Gill grinned suddenly from ear to ear. "The cricket? Oh, it was marvellous. Absolutely thrilling! The ball was being hit everywhere, even into the river, and the catching was amazing. I didn't open my book once. Glamorgan looked very dashing in bright red pyjamas; while, I thought, Somerset came across somewhat negatively in their black. But I suppose that was just me expecting whites, 'cos Somerset weren't negative at all! The tannoy blared out 'Glamorgan-morgan-morgan' a few times but it seemed very feeble compared to Jeremy constantly balling 'Somerset la-la-la' in his deep operatic bass."

Gill took an intake of breath. "I loved how Pollard held his pose for three or four seconds after he hit a six. And next week Jeremy and I've planned to go and watch Somerset play Hampshire. I'm sure that will be fantastic, too. Hopefully Jeremy'll have his voice back by then."

"Yay!" I enthused.

"Cricket's wonderful, isn't it? And guess what?"

"What?"

"I've agreed to proof-read that book."

"Jolly good!" Holy moly, Gill was more of a convert than my wife. "How did Fisher John get on? I can't imagine he let himself get too excited."

"Oh, he didn't go in the end. He decided to go fishing, instead."

"I used to be like that, but thankfully I grew out it. All power to the ladies, eh?"

Somerset v Hampshire

County Ground, Taunton on 9 July 2010 (20-over match).
Umpires: PJ Hartley, D J Millns.
Hampshire won toss and decided to bat.

Hampshire Innings

Adams	c Pollard	b Turner	21
Carberry	run out (Trescothick)		3
Vince		b B Phillips	22
McKenzie	lbw	b Thomas	73
Ervine	c Ben Phillips	b Trego	53
Razzaq		not out	27
Christian			8
Extras 2nb 5w 2lb			9
Total		for 5	216 (20 overs)

Fall of wickets: 1-4, 2-42, 3-57, 4-169, 200-McKenzie

Did not bat: Pothas (W), Cork (C), Wood, Briggs, Christian.

Somerset Innings

Trescothick	c and b	Briggs	78
Trego		not out	72
Pollard	c Ervine	b Briggs	0
Hildreth		run out	29
de Bruyn	c Adams	b Christian	6
Buttler		not out	18
Extras 2nb 2w 5b 8lb		17	
Total		for 4	220 (18 overs)

Fall of wickets: 1-116, 2-116, 3-154, 4-166

Did not bat: Suppiah, B Phillips, Thomas, Kartik, Turner.

Man of the Match: ME Trescothick's innings lasted 27 balls during which he hit 7 fours and 7 sixes. His 50 came in 13 balls in just 17 minutes with 5 fours and 5 sixes.

Somerset won by 6 wickets.

Bitten Nails and Pennant Dreams

"You see things; and you say, 'Why?' But I dream
things that never were; and I say, 'Why not?'"
George Bernard Shaw (Irish Playwright and Essayist, 1856-1950).

For a few weeks now aging Somerset members had been sensing the extraordinary actually happening in their lifetimes. Like cats on hot bricks, coins jingling in their pockets, they made queues behind Taunton's car park ticketing machines before finally being able to leg it, anticipatory and jaunty, towards the Sir Vivian Richards gates. The Championship dream beckoned and, just to be greedy, there was the Clydesdale Bank 40 final to look forward to as well. Amongst the throng I was sprightly, too, infected by the mood of heady days. They were to become changeable in more ways than one after Durham's near end of season arrival at the County Ground.

"He's all desire and effort. Wish we had eleven of him," said one twinkled-eyed, old Somerset member with a love of chatting to folk and who never sat down, preferring instead to just walk around the ground. I followed his gaze to Mark Turner. But not everyone thought like that veteran supporter. Much later, in the bar of Taunton's *Picture and Piano* Mark was gently interrupted. He had been catching up on past times with Graham Onions whom he had been at school with when the 'D-word' was whispered – Derbyshire.

The sudden morose nod of Mark's popular head confirmed it was more than a rumour. After the Clydesdale Bank 40 final he would join the exodus to what Somerset supporters now joked as being the Somerset Second Eleven. One of the nicest blokes you would ever want to meet, and one who enjoyed a little sea-fishing whenever he got the chance, would be shortly on the path trod in the past by Fred Rumsey, Andy Hayhurst and Charl Langeveldt and more recently by salad dodging Steffan Jones and the erstwhile Unicorn, Wes Durston. Not just Somerset, but Taunton St. Andrews, too, would miss 'Tina'.

A week later, Max Waller, chuffed to still be on the Somerset books, had got his hopes up of getting a game. The pitch it was thought might be a turner. Mark Turner played. Max, although "a bit pissed off", could only shrug and admit that Somerset cricket was all about being part of a squad and if things might get misinterpreted occasionally not a lot could be done in retrospect.

Somerset had lost the final. BBC Somerset's sports commentator Rob Scanlon probably felt relieved he'd been assigned to do Redbridge versus Bristol Rovers rather than the cricket ball-to-ball. The heroic bowling efforts of Ben Phillips had been in vain as Warwickshire centurian Ian Bell, recovered from a foot injury sustained on England duty, had seen the ball like a beach ball and unfortunately chose to pick on Mark Turner.

Now the dew was well settled, the floodlights of Lord's had been switched off and somewhere in the September dark of Saturday the 18th 2010 Marcus Trescothick ordered an expensive round of Jägermeister. That was just for starters, the beginnings of what would by the night's end exceed two grand from out of his own pocket. Marcus and his Somerset team, together with their small entourage, were in a dimly lit London nightclub, the bouncers of which Nick Compton had become acquainted with during his spell at Middlesex. Nick, Somerset's top scorer earlier in the day, had managed to wangle both tickets and tables. Marcus's intoxicating gesture was as a thank you to his team's efforts over the season despite the bitter disappointment of missing out at the last gasp on not one, but three trophies.

Those in their order were the Friends Provident T20, losing on the last ball of the Final against Hampshire; the LV County Championship, coming runners up as Nottinghamshire edged it with forty minutes of the season remaining having finished level on points but winning one game more than Somerset; and forty-eight hours later, the Clydesdale Bank 40, losing by a margin of three wickets. One was happy to relate therefore that in the pervading gloom Somerset discovered the healing powers of laughter.

Close by, and each wearing a pair of dark designer shades, the music phenomenons rapper Tinchy Stryder and the R&B singer Taio Cruz held court to an entourage of possibly nigh on a hundred glamour chicks in the nightclub's VIP lounge.

The sight caused one waggish West Countryman to reduce his cricketing teammates into a fit of mirth by loudly posing the question: "Hey mates, where's the bloomin' sunshine?"

At the same time back in Wivey, at the timeworn pub tables in the 'Bearin' Up', the post-mortems were by now well under way. The failures, should they have been unjustly described as such, had been by whiskers, and those whiskers must have belonged to my very petite cat.

Joined in dribs and drabs by those returning from their trip to St John's Wood most bibblers just sighed, others were inconsolable. The guddlers simply drank their sorrows into insensibility. Not a soul felt any anger with the Somerset team. And surely that was the reality across the length and breadth of Somerset. If anything, the devotion felt to the county side was full to over-flowing. For us supporters it had been tough going, both mentally and phys-ically.

Mooseman and I both admitted to suffering from bitten nails as we exchanged philosophical notes on where things, in our humble opinions, had gone so desperately wrong.

"A black eye, old Nick, and that Christian." This was Mooseman's explana-tion for the Rose Bowl's mid-August day of soggy wet balls, the culmination of the T20 competition that had seen Alfonso Thomas win so many "Man of the Match" awarded cheques that, he joked, they paid for his new Audio TT.

The black eye belonged to Kieron Pollard. Missing the ball with his bat he had his right eye closed by a short pitch exocet from Dominic Cork causing my wife to jump from her seat with a shout aimed at Dominic of "You brutish man!" So instead of having a bowl at Hampshire Kieron had to go to hospi-tal. After the final he was found at three o'clock in the morning in tears in his hotel room, feeling he had let everybody down.

During the chaotic ten minutes of the match's last over bowled by Zander de Bruyn Somerset had several opportunities to win, yet took none of them. Craig Kieswetter played skittles twice and was agonisingly awry both times. Nick Compton dropped a boundary catch, a sitter, before a groundsman was summoned to mark out a runner's crease. "Whitewash! Whitewash!" was the cry. On the groundsman trotted, a bucket in one hand, and in his other a piece of straight edge timber and a brush. This must have been a distraction for, to cap it all in the final ball fever, Somerset forgot they could run out Dan Christian who looked like a panda having been hit in the face by a ball by de Bruyn a couple of days earlier. He charged down the pitch for the vital single, absent-minded that it was he who had the runner.

Even then Mooseman had done his best for an Umpire's review screaming "Hampshire's on the pitch, the whole Hampshire team's on the bloody pitch. They're not allowed to be on the pitch. The match isn't officially over. Umpire!" Technically Mooseman was right. The Hampshire players did run onto the field before the final ball stopped rolling, thereby making it a 'dead' ball. Unfortunately, his protests went unheard as he was shouting at his sitting room telly.

Nodding with understanding I chipped in other noteworthy highlights. Kieron's leaping catch at long on to win the semi-final was probably the best of the season. And then there was the hilarity of the fire alarm in the BBC commentary box that caused Alison Mitchell to commentate via roving mic from the terrace of the stand sans headphones with many a tuned-in spectator waving at her, including six giant bananas doing a conga beneath the scoreboard and Snow White and seven Grumpies. The way Ms. Mitchell carried on, I could have sworn her sympathies lay with Hampshire. But at least Frampo had won his bet with Marcus.

Andrew Frampton of the internet radio station *Farm Radio* bet that if he got on the pitch at the toss on that final's day Marcus would in return open the new pavilion of Frampo's local village team in Dorset. Come the toss and much to the Somerset captain's surprise Frampo did duly arrive. Looking very official, dressed in a smart blazer and carrying a clipboard having hoodwinked the Rose Bowl security he reportedly whispered in Marcus's ear, "Here I am – now you come and open our pavilion."

However, it was the County Championship and the desolation of what might have that caused the greatest heartache. People were getting excited – some planned to jump on flights north.

A rheumy-eyed Brian Rose had tried to put a brave face on his sadness at Chester-le-Street after Durham, Ian Blackwell et al, had forced a draw while Lancashire capitulated to Notts, something that caused a Lancashire supporter to blog an embarrassed "Sorry" and wrote his intent not to renew his club membership, giving solidarity to the view that Somerset remains just about everyone's second favourite county cricket team.

And actually things had begun to get really exciting when Lancashire had been the visitors for Somerset's last home Championship game of the season. The growing tension was apparent. "The guys are well aware of the history of the club and never winning the championship," Marcus had told BBC Somerset, before adding stuff about still having "a massive mountain to climb".

During a last wicket partnership between Murali Kartik and Charl

Willoughby, under oppressively black rain threatening clouds, the lead was extended to 123. Murali hit his second fifty of the campaign. Charl, too, hit some lusty blows, including the flattest of sixes, and he would later tweet "I will be a proper allrounder if I get to 1000 1st class runs and 850 wickets!" Then so, so close to an extra batting point Charl was run out while on what can only be described as a meandering ornithological survey of seagulls. "Ooer," said an affable 'red-roser' standing beside me. "That dropped batting point might just be the one that mattered. Lanky-Lanky-Lancashire!"

"I think what mattered," I said, interrupting his flow, "was losing our first two games of the season. Then again, if we cider boys do win the title, due thanks must be given to Yorky Jacques Rudolph for his quixotically generous declaration back in May. He rather put the white-rosers Championship hopes on the back-burner here."

"Oh well, good luck to you. I only came today to watch Chanderpaul bat."

Others wanted to watch, too. About to start his two-hour stint of duty, stood in front of the Old Pavilion steps but behind the canvas sightscreen, a grey-bearded safety-steward friend in a floppy summer hat rather dilly-dallied. He wished he had a pair of scissors about his person to cut a small hole through which he could eyeball the unfolding drama.

As it turned out Shivnarine Chanderpaul didn't last too long. Alfonso Thomas claimed his wicket and it was key to Somerset winning the match. It also earned him a prize – a choice of one of Marcus's bats. "I went over to his bat corner before the season started and asked him what I had to do to get one," said Alfonso told the local press. "He said get me one hundred wickets and you can take your pick." The gifted West Indian falling ell bee took Alfonso's tally past the hundred mark in all competitions for the season.

However, it wasn't the prospect of a beautiful bat that pleased Alfonso most. "If you'd said to us at the beginning of the season, two points behind with the last game to go I think we would have chopped off both arms really," he had enthused. On hearing this, and having witnessed the great Alfonso being caught by a Sky Sports camera on the Somerset balcony dragging on a fag, Mooseman confided in me that the chopping-the-arm-off business might eventually come regardless, if the whippet-like bowler didn't quit his naughty smoking habit.

Ironically, the Fates conspired that it should be Shivnarine Chanderpaul edging to a gleeful Nottinghamshire slip that would ultimately signal a helicopter to whisk the Championship trophy to Trent Bridge. What had happened further north before that fateful moment lay recorded in my Moleskine. I passed the notebook over to Mooseman for him to have a gander at.

Monday 13 September
11.00 am Rain.
3.25 pm Play underway.

Durham 132 for 2 at close.

Evening. Brian Rose, Vic Marks and Somerset President Roy Kerslake dine at the *Fat Buddha* a restaurant of Asian fusion offering "high design and unique atmosphere". They discuss Twenty20, the acquisition of Steve Kirby from Gloucestershire and drainage.

Tuesday 14 September
11.00 am Somerset supporters are getting excited – some have planned to jump on flights to Newcastle. BBC forecasting the following for the next 3 days:

Manchester - 2 days of rain.
Durham - SUNSHINE FOR 3 DAYS! GAME ON!

2.30 pm Third bowling point and Somerset lead the county championship table by one point – clear skies over Chester-le-Street. Sodden outfield prevents play at Old Trafford.

Set of rain clouds heading inland from Welsh coast. If a biblical storm were to arrive on these shores and wipe out all cricket from now until Thursday night Somerset would be county champions for the first time.

2.32 pm Ben Phillips traps debutant Raul Brathwaite lbw. Durham 286 all out.

4.48 pm Bad light and late afternoon rain.

5.00 pm Durham Scoreboard switched off, scorer gone home.

5.15 pm Scorer probably has to do a U-turn in rush-hour traffic. Tresco and Compton restart the Somerset innings.

6.05 pm Somerset lead Championship by 2 points. Pete Trego tucks a single off his ribs.

Somerset supporters from Toronto, Daar al Salam, and Instanbul blog they're going potty. In Bejing a supporter was teaching flatmates "Somerset La-La-La" in basic Mandarin.

6.10 pm Ian Blackwell - hands in pockets, two sweaters, looking absolutely perished, rubbed the ball to polish it and drops it. Bless. In Manchester, Notts have only managed to reach 89 for 2 after two days.

Wednesday 15 September
11.00 pm Blue skies in the North East. Somerset resume day three on 226-4.

12.55 pm Ben Harmison traps both Jos Buttler and Ben Phillips ell bee to the last two balls before lunch.
1.40 pm Rain stops play.

2.10 pm Players back on.

2.30 pm James Hildreth pulls Liam Plunkett for four. Hildreth 100! Great advert for Millfield School. His 7th century of season and he gets married within the week.

2.38 pm The Great Alfonso nurdles 3 runs. Somerset 400-7. Maximum batting points. 6 points clear at the top! Somerset become the first team to score 400 at Chester-le-Street in 2010.

3.05 pm Alfonso has his timbers tickled by Ruel Brathwaite. Somerset 423-9.

3.11 pm Murali Kartik skies a catch to Ian Blackwell to bring the Somerset innings to a close. The leaders are 426 all out and lead by 140. Tea.

6.00 pm Durham 171-2. Di Venuto hinders Somerset's victory push. Close. Somerset 8pts, Durham 5pts. Notts still frustrated by the Manchester puddles. No play during day.

'Stuart', a Notts supporter clutching at straws blogged the following: "What are the ethics, rules or laws around Notts and Lancashire concocting some sort of result? Personally I'd be up for some skulduggery, but I'm the sort of bloke who doesn't walk when he nicks it."

Thursday 16 September
Manchester: Notts hit 311 runs in squelch after a delayed start, closing their first innings on 400 for 9. 5 batting points. Sugarplums!

Somerset draw. I bite nails. Pennant dreams now hang on the bats of the red rose top order.

6.30 pm Blog: "As a member of Lancashire CCC all I can do is offer my sincere apologies for our spineless surrender today, sad to say it's not the first time it's happened this season. All in all a gutless batting exhibition less than 5 overs to lose 3 wickets. Sorry. Somerset had a right to expect something better."

Had 'Stuart' been merely mischievous yesterday?

Mooseman snapped my Moleskine shut and unwittingly put it down in a table puddle of spilt cider. "What a bloody cryin' shame," he said, obviously speaking of the cricket. "Ah well, I'm sure they'll be up for trying again next year bolstered with a few new faces."

I dried the Moleskine with a grotty tissue. "Yep, true. Although, sat in land-locked Derbyshire, Mark Turner will miss his sea-fishing."

The following morning as the bronze impacts of church bells bim-bommed few folk seemed to going to pray any thanks to the Lord. And somewhere nearby, perhaps startled from a Wurzel tree, a blackbird chack-chack-chacked. For my part, I read Vic Marks's thoughts on the Championship race in Sunday's *Observer*. They were few and simple. "The delicious agony of waiting continues in the West Country."

New Bats and Golden Leaves

*"We all have our time machines. Some take us back, they're called memories.
Some take us forward, they're called dreams."*

Jeremy Irons (British actor).

Nobody seemed to care about the score, or about leaving the black metal plates with their white painted numbers strewn across the boundary edge grass, nor about the easel perched scoreboard, nor indeed about the huggermugger of helmets, gloves, bats, pads and fag ends. The scene played out before the eye was too much of a distraction.

The resident pooches had been joined by the famous 'Mad Dog'.

To the ignorance of nearby blackberry pickers, Wivey's cricket season came to an abrupt close as sporting interest in the last match prematurely waned in favour of rugby with the unexpected appearance of Lewis Moody and a bunch of his mates having a kickabout in the corner of the Recreation Ground with, Heaven forbid, a round football. Questions had to be asked, and Wivey's fielders, understandably nonplussed, deserted their positions to ask them.

Being Somerset rugby country the coming of the 'golden one' could be explained. The shape of ball could not. It transpired the England rugby captain had been staying at a local pub for a stag weekend. Waterrow made a such change from Tallinn, Riga or Prague.

For the umpires it had already been a disrupted afternoon. Minutes earlier the

Combine Harvester had been such an on-field irritation as to cause a mid-over conference. Now the gentleman who had been fielding with a mobile with the Wurzels ring tone in the pocket of his grass stained whites made a call. And by the time Lewis had autographed pre-school Charlie's first and most precious rugby ball, and Bugsy made the suggestion that the rugby posts be put up there and then, the visitors in whites could only shrug, put away their cricketing paraphernalia, and accept an honorable draw.

And elsewhere across Somerset the last hoick was hoicked to the many cow corners, the last clout clouted to Brompton Ralph's bullock bottom, and last splash of leather disturbed the Exe at Bridgetown.

So with that having been that, until the following spring October's leaves of copper and burnished gold were being blown across the County Ground's car park and being caught by windscreens. The chill caused me to shiver before I found autumnal sanctuary in Taunton's oldest complete building, the Priory Barn – aka the Somerset cricket museum.

The likable petite lady, wrinkled as a windfall apple adorned with a smear of red lipstick, was undoubtedly in charge. "If you want to come back again don't bother coming until 10.45 although the leaflet information says we open at 10.30, because I'll probably still be in bed," she tells visitors. Other things of a personal nature she kept to herself.

The first time I met her she declared that she wouldn't tell her name to a stranger, it was something she hadn't done since she was seventeen. A hint to her age came with her admission of frustratingly tackling the accounts of Somerset farmers for forty-two years. She forever turned farmers away, insisting they only come back once they found their cheque stubs and receipts. And there was also the story of her having been an amateur photographer. She had snapped Sammy Woods' pristine gravestone for inclusion in Clifford Jiggens' biography of the Somerset character. This must have been long before the prodigious growth of moss and lichen of today made the inscription unintelligible. However, she didn't object to me calling her 'Poppy' on account that she was wearing a red paper one on a green plastic stem in aid of the Remembrance Day appeal.

"Marcus Trescothick's in the window," she had announced somewhat alarmingly on my first visit, pointing at a commemorative, lidded wassailing cup that at first glace could be mistaken for an urn. My closer inspection of the exhibit sitting on the window ledge of the narrow leaded window showed the stone and clay cup, its lid topped by a set of stumps, was made by Frank Merton to celebrate Marcus's benefit year in 2008. Behind the cup lay a row of conkers. There were thirteen. Quizzical, I asked Poppy whether they related to any of Marcus's post-season pastimes.

"Oh, they were left by a lady. Apparently they keep spiders away."

I directed her attention to several industrious webs in the window's corners.

Poppy huffed. "Well, that's what they're supposed to be about – so nuts to it."

On that day of falling leaves Poppy left me to my own devices to greet the arrival of what looked like a retired Somerset farmer. Small, rosy cheeked, with gentle eyes and a nervous smile, he wore a flat cap and polished brown shoes, and leant on a varnished bamboo cane walking stick. He had obviously made every effort to look smart for the occasion. And he was proudly carrying a bat, its rubber handle grip perished, its blade protected in a very old brown paper sleeve that declared in bold blue lettering "Stuart Sturridge & Co. Ltd., Practical Sports Good Manufacturers, Contactors to the War Office, Admiralty, R.A.F., & L.C.C. Etc.".

The farmer type cleared his throat before addressing Poppy. "I brought this along. As my grandchildren weren't interested I thought the museum might like it. It's been in my attic for years."

"We've got so many bats," said Poppy a bit too abruptly, perhaps influenced by her experience of agricultural accounting. "We haven't room for any more. Sorry."

Be nice, Poppy, I thought to myself, Vic Mark's dad was a farmer from Middle Chinnock. Indeed, now a stalwart of Test Match Special and cricket writer for the *Observer* and *Guardian*, Vic had from time to time known to mutter about cricketing weather being "too dry for potatoes and too wet for wheat".

Poppy's farmer type, although downcast by her rebuttal, made another attempt to tempt. "But it's got all the names of the Somerset team signed on it."

"Sorry, no. I can't take it." That was Poppy's final word on the matter.

Out of pure interest I butted in. "Excuse me," I said, "Can I have a look?"

The farmer type obligingly passed me the bat and I slipped it out of its paper sleeve. "Ooo," I breathed. "Have you got time to have a chat with me, sir?" I asked the farmer type, who's name transpired to be Trevor, a retired poultry farmer from Godney. I gathered that he never really had much time to watch Somerset play cricket. Although in his teens he had managed to get to a couple of games at Rowden Road in Wells with a mate, when that mate wasn't packing up eggs for *Suprema*. Trevor thought it "a pity" the Somerset team hadn't graced Rowden Road field since 1951, the year he had won the bat in a 'Harvest Home' raffle when he was nineteen. Which by mental maths made Trevor now seventy-eight.

The Sturridge was a signature bat and to my eyes, somewhat intriguing – a bit of history. Somerset names of the past were indeed there in autographs: SS Rogers, HL Hazell, HFT Buse, MF Tremlett, E Hill, FL Angell, J Lawrence, Roy Smith, Khan Mohammad, HW Stephenson, EP Robinson, Bill Andrews, A Wellard.

But there were also other names scratched in ink pen. The touring South Africa cricket team of '51 was also upon the bat, as well the teams of Warwickshire, Northants and Glamorgan – counties that, as with Somerset, the men of the Southern Hemisphere had played against during their '51 tour of England which the hosts ended up winning by three Tests to one.

The Somerset game took place at the beginning of August. South Africa's captain Dudley Norse, a chap who by the time of his retirement held the highest batting average of any South African batsman and currently surpassed only by Jacques Kallis and Graeme Pollock, won the toss and decided to bat.

All went surprisingly well for Somerset until they managed to rather muck things up by squandering a first innings lead of 70 and losing by 24 runs after being all out second time around for 86 – an innings in which Les Angell and Johnny Lawrence shared a top score of 18 with Khan Mohammad not out on 10, an improvement on his first innings duck.

A year later Mohammad was to achieve fame in his home country as a cricketing pioneer. He bowled the first delivery and took the first wicket in Pakistan's inaugural Test match against India in Delhi. Oddly, in 1956 he played for Torquay. On his death in London in the summer of 2009 Pakistan Cricket Board chairman Ijaz Butt paid tribute, describing Mohammad as "Pakistan's outstanding fast bowler of the 1950s and a gentleman cricketer."

Somerset's first innings lead against South Africa was largely attributable to captain Stuart Rogers hitting 107. Gentle, buck-toothed smiler Stuart, his short hair cropped in fashionable striking waves, who survived fighting with the Chindits in the Burmese jungle during the War, and one of Somerset's last amateur skippers, was to die too young aged forty-six. If the rumour mill held water he was a bit of a guddler. Teammates who faced Dudley Norse's lot could attest to the accusation.

Somerset's senior professional, Horace Hazell, when taken out for drinks at restaurants by Stuart, returned "as drunk as a handcart". And Eric Hill, one of the younger players, recorded his skipper ordering a curfew of 10 o'clock, plotting his evening accordingly and staggering up to bed at half-past nine "more drunk than anyone I've ever seen in my life." In the match against South Africa, however, Stuart excelled himself by surpassing his previous highest first-class score of 101.

Counterbalancing Stuart was Bertie Buse in his twilight years at Somerset. John Arlott described Bertie's run-up was "like a butler bringing in the tea," while David Foot recorded in *Somerset Cricket: A Post-War Who's Who* that "there was rather too much posterior".

I looked up from the bat to Trevor. "Would you like me to find your bat a good home?"

Trevor nodded. I promised him the bat would be well looked after, and we shook hands on it as he departed but not before throwing an unhappy glance towards Poppy.

With the Sturridge beside me I decided to discover what other excitements happened in '51 away from the first-class scene. In the museum's library I found a worn, much dog-eared club yearbook to peruse. Leafing through I stumbled across the knowledge that there had been some Missfits from Weston-super-Mare – which was unsurprising I thought as today the town's said to be the rehab centre of Europe – and in addition the old county asylum Tone Vale Hospital, having beaten Bristol Mental Hospital, had lost to Taunton Old Crocks.

This latter enlightenment reminded me of an occasionally told tale of Somerset cricketers attending, it's said, a lively dance night at Tone Vale. A gentleman, with a daffodil sticking from one ear, kept warning the cricketers to beware of the other patients as they were all "raving lunatics".

My frivolous research was suddenly interrupted by the knocking sound reminiscent of a methodical woodpecker. Was 'Poppy' playing conkers at her desk while waiting for the next visitor? No, her desk that sat between the museum's twin doors that bore small independent signs that declared 'Not Out' and 'Out' was unoccupied. Poppy was showing a visiting mother and young son the "easily missed" stump camera exhibit.

The knocking, I realised, came from the Willow Yard around the back of the museum. I decided to be nosy and brave the outside elements to look in on the creation of a new generation.

The noise of mallet on willow came through the open barn door of bat makers Millichamp & Hall, purveyors of "Cricket equipment of distinction". A small patch terrier affair on a long lead stood on its hind legs and sniffed with interest into a steel drum full of wood shavings. Ah, I thought nostalgically if not a little naively, local craftsmen using the finest of local raw materials to make weapons of mass destruction.

"Hello," I called out, and was greeted by an affable young chap sporting a severe Sonic the hedgehog haircut and faded green trackie top. "Can I help you?"

"That's not a Somerset accent," I said, "it lacks a certain burr."

Introducing himself as Rob Chambers, he smiled and explained he had picked up the twang from time spent with Australians and South Africans.

I remarked that it had been a day of encountering South African influence. Rob thought this unlikely as Charl Willoughby, Alfonso Thomas and even Craig Kieswetter had left for their holidays, and Zander de Bruyn had left for good; well, at least until he returned in due course with Surrey. I explained the influence was long prior to Jimmy Cook ,let alone Graeme Smith. Leaving it at that I turned Rob's attention to bats.

Describing himself as a 3-D sculptor, Stogursey-born master craftsman Rob hazarded a guess that there were as few as twenty bat makers left in England. Indeed, having looked around the Lord's Long Room during a bat-makers' function he reckoned that he knew all the attending faces and most of them were youngish. "People," Rob said, "expect a bat maker to be old and smoke a pipe, but it's really quite taxing work, and there's a five to seven year apprenticeship."

"My God!" I exclaimed, "That's longer than a doctor."

Then after scrutinising me up and down, Rob assured me that he could make a bespoke bat for anyone – whatever their size – in an hour whilst keeping 'the client' in conversation. The end result would cost about £300.

"How much?!" I had exclaimed. Rob didn't flinch. If I wanted something cheaper than a 'M&H' there were bats being made in India by blokes earning a fiver a day. I thought of the embarrassment caused to me by a certain 'Hero' and winced.

With the terrier having lost complete interest in the drum of shavings I enquired whether the shavings were all Somerset willow. Rob shook his head.

"None of them. There's little Somerset willow available. Our willow's supplied by the Essex wholesalers' R Goodwin & Sons. They've got the market sewn up and buy directly from landowners. Anyway, getting bat wood out of the tree is an art in itself."

What I really wanted to know was which of the current crop of Somerset players did he make bats for? The answer, he replied, was confidential. Players had restrictions placed on them by sponsors. And there were all sorts of endorsements between the player and whichever company was willing to swell the player's bank account. But Rob did confide that he had made bats for Justin Langer and Sachin Tendulkar.

Had he make Ben Phillips' bat? I had noticed towards the season's end that Ben's bat was boringly plain, bereft of jazzy logos or even the bat-maker's name. Rob shrugged. Ben had simply bust his own and had to borrow one from another player. Who? Well, that was another secret. It was quite common for that sort of thing to go on when the team was on the road. But yes, Rob had made Ben's bat and it was the heaviest on the county circuit – and his tool to achieve the second highest strike rate, a plunder which earned him an interview with Sky Sports. There were certainly regrets among Somerset supporters that Ben had been let go and that, ironically, the following season he would be tied up with Notts playing his cricket beneath the dreamed of Championship pennant fluttering above Trent Bridge.

But it was time for me to hit the road away from the Taunton's County Ground, too.

Later that afternoon back home behind my warped, blue front door I removed Trevor's bat once more from its sleeve and played a few fanciful shots at make-belief balls. As I saved the day for Somerset I conjured to mind RC Robinson-Glasgow's words from *All in the Game*:

"What does it matter if it was all a legend? As the years lend enchantment to the days of youth, the runs and the wickets of the imagination are as good as any that illuminate the pages of *Wisden*."

After thirteen and a half decades of Somerset history bring on next season with its kit bags of bats, pads and cider.

SOMERSET v SOUTH AFRICANS 1951

County Ground, Taunton on 1, 2, 3 August 1951 (3-day match).

South Africans won the toss and decided to bat.

South Africans first innings

DJ McGlew	c and b Hazell	68
+JHB Waite	lbw b Buse	3
WR Endean	st Stephenson b Lawrence	13
*AD Nourse	b Khan Mohammad	4
JE Cheetham	b Khan Mohammad	36
GM Fullerton	st Stephenson b Hazell	13
PNF Mansell	c Rogers b Buse	62
HJ Tayfield	c Angell b Lawrence	3
NBF Mann	b Lawrence	2
GWA Chubb	c Stephenson b Khan Mohammad	22
MG Melle	not out	4
Extras (5 nb)		5
Total (all out, 71.5 overs)		235

Fall of wickets:
1-9, 2-42, 3-49, 4-121, 5-129, 6-161, 7-166, 8-178, 9-227, 10-235 (71.5 ov)

Bowling: Khan Mohammad: 19-1-74-3; Buse: 16.5-4-43-2;
     Lawrence: 17 –1-67-3; Hazell: 19 –4-46-2.

Somerset first innings

FL Angell	lbw	b Mansell	9
E Hill		b Mansell	34
J Lawrence	lbw	b Mann	3
MF Tremlett	lbw	b Chubb	41
HFT Buse		b Melle	46
R Smith		b Chubb	0
*SS Rogers		not out	107
Khan Mohammad		b Melle	0
+HW Stephenson		c Mansell b Mann	17
HL Hazell		b Melle	29
EP Robinson		c Endean b Chubb	13
Extras (1 b, 3 lb, 2 nb)			6
Total (all out, 96.5 overs)			305

Fall of wickets:

1-33, 2-46, 3-58, 4-106, 5-106, 6-177, 7-177, 8-221, 9-288, 10-305 (96.5 ov)

Bowling: Melle: 13-0-5-9-3; Chubb: 28.5-3-99-3; Mansell: 17- 3-59-2; Mann: 31-14-70-2; Tayfield: 7-3-12-0.

South Africans second innings

DJ McGlew		b Khan Mohammad	0
+JHB Waite		b Khan Mohammad	18
WR Endean		lbw b Robinson	17
*AD Nourse	c Robinson	b Hazell	31
JE Cheetham		lbw b Robinson	62
GM Fullerton	c Lawrence	b Robinson	20
PNF Mansell	c Stephenson	b Hazell	0
HJ Tayfield	c Buse	b Robinson	2
NBF Mann	c Lawrence	b Hazell	14
GWA Chubb		lbw b Robinson	4
MG Melle		not out	0
Extras (4 b, 7 lb, 1 nb)			12
Total (all out, 69.2 overs)			180

Fall of wickets:
1-6, 2-26, 3-47, 4-95, 5-136, 6-137, 7-150, 8-166, 9-180, 10-180 (69.2 ov)

Bowling: Khan Mohammad: 9-4-30-2; Buse: 8-1-13-0; Hazell: 26.2-4-66-3; Robinson: 26-7-59-5.

Somerset second innings

FL Angell		run out	18
E Hill	c Waite	b Chubb	1
J Lawrence	c Mansell	b Chubb	18
MF Tremlett	c sub	b Chubb	11
HFT Buse	c Waite	b Chubb	0
R Smith		lbw b Chubb	5
*SS Rogers		b Mann	7
Khan Mohammad		not out	10
+HW Stephenson		b Mann	0
HL Hazell	c Mansell	b Mann	4
EP Robinson		b Mann	6
Extras (2 b, 3 lb, 1 nb)			6
Total (all out, 43.3 overs)			86

Fall of wickets:
1-2, 2-35, 3-50, 4-50, 5-55, 6-64, 7-66, 8-66, 9-72, 10-86 (43.3 ov)

Bowling: Melle: 3-0-15-0; Chubb: 14- 5-21-5; Mansell: 2-2-0-0;
Mann: 17.3-6-30-4; Tayfield: 7-3-14-0.

South Africans won by 24 runs.

"I can't think of a life without cricket."

Sanath Jayasuriya,
Sri Lanka and Somerset.

Rain Stopped Play

NINETEEN

A Bit of Head Scratching

"The heart that truly loves never forgets."
Proverb.

1. In 1935 Harold Gimlett was Somerset's first winner of the Walter Lawrence Trophy for scoring the fastest century in a season. Name the other three winners who won the trophy whilst playing for the county. And for extra brownie points give the dates.

2. The old River Stand was provided by the supporters' club formed in 1953 to give help to the cricket club. How was the money mainly raised?
a. A football competition.
b. A rugby competion.
c. Greyhound racing.
d. Sponsored cycling.

3. What is the length of the longest hit ever made by a Somerset player at Lord's and who hit it?
a. 132.2 yards (120.0 metres) by Kieron Pollard.
b. 157.0 yards (143.6 metres) by William Fowler.
c. 145.4 yards (133,0 metres) by Cuthbert Fairbanks-Smith.
d. 161.0 yards (147.2 metres) by Charles Sweet.

4. Name the Somerset bowler who broke West Indies' captain Jimmy Adam's cheek bone.

5. The shortest time in which a first-class county match has ever been completed involved Somerset. Against whom did they play? And when?

6. Name the Somerset bowler who was no-balled before he had loosed his hold of the ball which, in fact, was not delivered:

a. Len Braund.
b. Bryan Lobb.
c. Maurice Tremlett.
d. Adrian Jones.

7. Name the Somerset player who hit the last ball of the last over clean out of the ground to win the match on the stroke of time?

a. Norman Mitchell-Innes.
b. Bunty Longrigg.
c. Ernie Robson.
d. Colin McCool.

8. Which two Somerset batsman shared a stand of 197 for the first wicket as Somerset beat the Australians at Taunton in June 2005?

9. In 1929 Ronald Gywnne Seldon took all ten wickets in a two-day match against the Somerset Stragglers, hitting the stumps seven times, for 70 runs and scored 100 not out on the same day. Who was Ronald playing for?

a. Glamorgan Dragons.
b. Sussex Martlets.
c. Devon Dumplings.
d. Cornish Pirates.

10. Robert Dixon Burrows, a fast bowler playing against Somerset at Taunton bowled with all but two of his team's eleven arranged in a semi-circle, from deep point to the wicket-keeper, each of them close enough to shake hands with his neighbour. Who was Robert playing for?

a. Nottinghamshire.
b. Worcestershire.
c. Kent.
d. Derbyshire.

11. On 28 August, 1946, the first day of the Somerset v. Derbyshire match at Frome, a most unusual incident occurred due to the tempestuous, foul weather. What was it?

a. A marquee was blown across the wicket.
b. The Derbyshire wicket-keeper caught a mallard duck in his gloves.
c. The captains and umpires agreed for players to wear galoshes.
d. The captains and umpires agreed to play without bails.

12. Crescens Robinson nicknamed 'the White Mouse' because of his complexion and hair, was an unorthodox tailender who gained notoriety for once having doing what?
a. Stuck his tongue out at the umpire for turning down an ell bee appeal.
b. Kicked the ball to the boundary.
c. Ate a cheese sandwich on his way to the wicket after tea.
d. Had his trousers fall down when going for a run.

13. Of which overseas player that played a single match for Somerset in 2001 was it said, "Players like that are no good to our club. In fact, no good for any club. He's a superstar and just does what he wants?"

14. Two Hallams played for Somerset. Hallam Moseley was one. Name the other.

15. Special Somerset guest at the Clydesdale Bank 40 final at Lord's in 2010, name the player who was Man of the Match of the Cheltenham and Gloucester Trophy final in 2001 and captained both Taunton St Andrew's and the Unicorns.

16. Against which county did Somerset declare after one over with the score 1-0 in a one-day game? And when?

17. Which Somerset player was it said could swear for five minutes without repeating himself?
a. Reggie Ingle.
b. Brian Close.
c. Horace Hazell.
d. Colin McCool.

18. Which Somerset player, later to become head groundsman and cricket coach at King's College, Taunton, where he helped hone the skills of Jos Buttler, was described as "a bag of nerves"?

19. In 1954 Harold Stephenson was awarded the Brylcreem Cup. For what?

20. Which Somerset player is said to have owned neither sprinkler or watering can, and, instead, watered his garden plants from a frying pan and serenaded his favourite blooms with "Blowin' in the Wind"?
a. Graham Rose.
b. Peter Roebuck.
c. Keith Dutch.
d. Nixon McLean.

21. Which Somerset player became the Carling Single Wicket Cricket Champion in 1963?
a. Ken Palmer.
b. Bill Alley.
c. Colin Atkinson.
d. Roy Virgin.

22. Who having showed rare talent as a batsman and a wicket keeper won his first cap for England in 1997 and in 2010 was captain of Somerset playing disabled cricket?

23. On 20 June 1921 two players took ten wickets for their respective teams. A "bad boy" of cricket Billy Bestwick, miner, alcoholic, man of wild temperament and reckless behaviour, who incidentally killed a man in a pub brawl, was the toast of Derbyshire taking 10-40 against Glamorgan at Cardiff Arms Park. Who was the success story for Somerset with 10-76 against Worcestershire at New Road?
a. Harry Chidgey.
b. Ernie Robson.
c. John White.
d. George Hunt.

24. Which former Somerset wicketkeeper hit the winning runs for Ilminster when they won the Herbert Baker Memorial Cup at the County Ground in July 2010?
a. Trevor Gard.
b. Carl Gazzard.
c. Rob Turner.
d. Sam Spurway.

25. In Sir Arthur Conan Doyle's 1918 work *The New Revelation*, Doyle gives his own views and thoughts on the relationship between spiritual revelations and conventional religious dogma. Within the book he makes reference to a conversation held with a spirit he chooses to call Dodd. Doyle would later claim Dodd was which late Somerset cricketer?
a. John Trask.
b. Joe Ambler.
c. Stephen Newton.
d. Frederick Poynton.

26. Which overseas batsman was replaced by Sunil Gavaskar in 1980?
a. Jimmy Cook.
b. Kepler Wessels.
c. Martin Crowe.
d. Jamie Cox.

27. Using a wind tunnel scientists tried unsuccessfully to discover why the ball with which Sir Ian Botham took five Australian wickets for one run in twenty-eight deliveries in 1981 had swung so prodigiously. Where were those experiments carried out?
a. Rolls Royce in Derby.
b. BAE Systems in Farnborough
c. Westland Helicopters in Yeovil
d. Saunders-Roe in East Cowes.

28. Televised by ITV, and with a winners cheque of £6000 presented by *World of Sport* presenter Dickie Davies, the inaugural Silk Cut Challenge was held at Taunton in September 1984. Who won it?
a. Kapil Dev.
b. Sir Richard Hadlee.
c. Sir Ian Botham.
d. Clive Rice.

29. Which club founded over 100 years ago and has always played its cricket on the Red Post ground, and once had a 2nd XI known as the "Old Blacks"?
a. Chew Magna.
b. Peasedown St John.
c. Butleigh.
d. Ashcott & Shapwick.

30. Somerset's highest score to date is 860 for 7 declared. In what year was this score achieved?

Answers in the Appendix

Appendix

Answers to a Bit of Head Scratching

1. Sir Vivian Richards 1980 and 1986, Sir Ian Botham 1982 and 1985, and Ian Blackwell 2005. The Walter Lawrence Trophy is awarded for the season's fastest century. Ian Blackwell's trophy-winning century was scored for Somerset against Derbyshire at Taunton, on the 24th of September 2005. The big-hitting, left-handed all-rounder survived two chances in the slips off successive balls when he had made 35 before racing to 107, with his hundred coming off 67 balls and including two sixes and eighteen fours. Two-times winner Ian Botham scored his first award winning century in 52 minutes in 1982 for Somerset playing against Warwickshire at Taunton. He won the Trophy for a second time in 1985. Two times winner Viv Richards scored his second award winning century in 1986 off 48 balls for Somerset playing against Glamorgan at Taunton. He won the trophy for the first time in 1980 again playing against a hapless Glamorgan.

2. a. A football competition.

3. 157 yards, by William Fowler v. MCC in 1882. Out of interest William was a banker who designed golf courses in Britain and America and who at the age of 24 lived at 1 Hammett Street, Taunton, unmarried, and was looked after by two domestic servants, Thomas Lapworth the butler and his wife Phoebe the cook. William's brothers Gerald and Howard also played for Somerset. Albert Trott's record of 1899 remains for the time being as the only batsman to ever *clear* the famous Lord's Pavilion, although Kieron Pollard came mighty close in June 2010. But for hitting the top of a protruding air-conditioning unit at the rear of the top terrace he would also have attained the feat.

4. Andre van Troost.

5. Middlesex v. Somerset, at Lord's, in May 1899, lasted only 3 hours and 5 minutes for Middlesex to win by an innings and 7 runs. Only 165 runs were scored for the loss of 30 wickets. Scores – Middlesex 86, Somerset 35 and 44.

6. Len Braund, bowling for Somerset v. Middlesex, at Lord's in June 1900. During the second innings of Middlesex, he was no-balled by H Pickett before he had loosed his hold on the ball. It was officially decided the decision must stand and a run be added to the total, although no such addition was at first made.

7. Ernie Robson v. Middlesex, a Weston-super-Mare, on 28 July, 1922. Aged fifty-one, he hit a six winning the match for Somerset by 2 wickets, at exactly 7 pm.

8. Graeme Smith and Sanath Jayasuriya. Set a target of 343, Somerset reached 345-6 with 19 balls to spare after Smith (108) and Jayasuriya (101) had shared a first-wicket stand of 197. Smith reached his century off 68 balls, with 17 fours. Jayasuriya struck three sixes and was only nine balls slower in reaching three figures. "The bowling and fielding was what made me angry," said the Australia captain Ricky Ponting who had a spell with Somerset the previous summer.

9. c. Devon Dumplings.

10. b. Worcestershire.

11. d. The captains and umpires agreed to play without bails.

12. b. Kicked the ball to the boundary.

13. Shoaib Akhtar, the Pakistani fast bowler.

14. Hallam Newton Egerton "Granny" Alston, He played one first-class cricket match for Somerset against Surrey at The Oval in 1933. While he scored just two runs in the first innings of the game and four in the second, his bowling figures of 1-6 from seven overs were economical, and his only first-class wicket was that of 50-year-old former Test cricketer Jack Hobbs, though Hobbs had made 117 by the time he was out.

15. Keith Parsons. In the 2001 final Somerset beat Leicestershire by 41 runs. Keith top scored with 60 runs and took two wickets.

16. Worcestershire. 23 May 1979. The match was at Worcestershire in the Group stage of the Benson and Hedges Cup. Brian Rose declared after the end of the first over to 'preserve' Somerset's net run rate. Somerset were thrown out of the competition for him doing it.

17. a. Reggie Ingle. A right-handed middle-order batsman, Ingle was a regular player in the Somerset side from 1927 to 1937, and became solicitor in Bath. He also played cricket for Cambridge University, but, somewhat surprisingly given his language, failed to win a blue.

18. Dennis Breakwell. Nicknamed "The Severed Nerve", Dennis was a slow left-armer who became an all-rounder as his career developed. He moved from Northamptonshire to Somerset in 1973, shared a flat in Taunton with Ian Botham and Viv Richards during Somerset's golden years, and was a key part of the Somerset side, appearing in two winning Lord's finals. Dennis has also pioneered schools coaching around Somerset.

19. Wicket keeping. In 1954 Harold had eighty-six victims. Fifty caught and thirty-six stumped.

20. Peter Roebuck.

21. a. Ken Palmer. He beat Middlesex's 'Knocker' White in the final. Knocker scored 7 before he was caught. Ken won after hitting 8 not out.

22. Julian Bellew. An information analyst for Somerset County Council, Julian was born with curvature of the spine and a separate muscle wasting disease. Disabled cricket has been in existence in England since 1991.

23. c. John White. Affectionately known as "Farmer'.

24. d. Sam Spurway. The winning runs were appropriately scored by Sam with a four to mid-wicket as Ilminster finished on 137-2 off 18.4 overs, the former Somerset wicket-keeper finishing unbeaten on 68.

25. a. John Trask. Trask was a Surgeon-Captain who made 16 first-class appearances for Somerset between 1884 and 1895. He died from cholera in Sudan during 1896. In his obituary appearing in the British Medical Journal no reference was made to his Somerset days, preferring to mention instead that he had been captain of the Gymkhana Cricket Eleven in Poona

26. b. Kepler Wessels.

27. c. Westland Helicopters in Yeovil. The tests were carried out at the instigation of Sir Ian Botham's late father Herbert, an aeronautical engineer.

28. d. Clive Rice. Kapil Dev was runner-up, Sir Ian Botham came 3rd, Sir Richard Hadlee 4th, and purely out of interest Malcolm Marshall came 5th.

29. b. Peasedown St John. In the very early days of this village set in the Somerset coalfield near Bath the local gentry formed the 1st XI and the local coal miners the 2nd XI. The miners were known as the 'Old Blacks' as they could not afford whites. During the 1920s the miners laid the present square on a bed of ashes from Braysdown Colliery. Gradually improved over the years it has become one of the finest squares in Somerset.

30. 2007. Somerset v. Middlesex at the County Ground, Taunton in April.

Somerset first innings

ME Trescothick	c Godleman	b Kartik	70
NJ Edwards	c Richardson	b Silverwood	9
*JL Langer		b Murtagh	315
JC Hildreth	c Compton	b Silverwood	116
CL White	st Nash	b Kartik	114
ID Blackwell	c sub	b Kartik	6
PD Trego		b Kartik	130
+SHP Spurway		not out	44
PS Jones		not out	1
AR Caddick		did not bat	
CM Willoughby		did not bat	
Extras (14 b, 17 lb, 12 nb, 2 w)			45
Total (7 wickets, declared, 178.3 overs			850

Fall of wickets:
1-25 (Edwards), 2-120 (Trescothick), 3-362 (Hildreth), 4-589 (White),
5-611 (Blackwell), 6-719 (Langer), 7-845 (Trego)

Middlesex 600 for 4 declared and 209 for 2.

The match was drawn.